nourishing
SUPERFOOD
BOWLS

nourishing
SUPERFOOD
BOWLS

**75 HEALTHY AND DELICIOUS GLUTEN-FREE MEALS
TO FUEL YOUR DAY**

LINDSAY COTTER

AASDN Certified Nutrition Specialist and
Founder of the blog Cotter Crunch

PAGE STREET
PUBLISHING CO.

PAGE STREET
PUBLISHING CO.

First published in 2018 by

Page Street Publishing Co.

27 Congress Street, Suite 105

Salem, MA 01970

www.pagestreetpublishing.com

Distributed by Macmillan, sales in Canada by The Canadian Manda Group.

21   20   19   18   2   3   4   5

ISBN-13: 978-1-62414-486-8

ISBN-10: 1-62414-486-1

Library of Congress Control Number: 2017956838

Cover and book design by Page Street Publishing Co.

Photography by Lindsay Cotter

Printed and bound in the United States

dedication

To my loving husband and parents: You all are my rock!
Thank you for believing in me, always.

Thank you to my readers who inspire me daily and
support my dreams. It's an honor!

contents

INTRODUCTION

I'm nicknamed the "Sherpa wife" or "Sherpa Cotter." And I'm sure you're wondering what that title is all about. Here's the story of how I became a Sherpa wife, and how these nourish bowls have literally fueled us for the journey of life.

You see, I'm the wife of a former New Zealand pro triathlete (aka the Kiwi Cotter). Even though I have a degree in nutrition, my true passion is in sports nutrition and gluten-free diets, which is why I am also part of the American Academy of Sports Dietitians and Nutritionists.

I would make and pack our food and carry it from race to race, traveling, training camps and literally everywhere. I was prepared to do whatever it took to get us the right nutrition and fuel we needed, and on a slim budget! This is where I got the name "Sherpa wife."

We've spent years figuring out what works and what doesn't work in regard to fuel, performance and meal planning. Our focus is on anti-inflammatory and recovery meals, superfood nutrients and other tasty allergy friendly recipes. Personally, I spent years trying to figure out my own health issues due to a parasite and gut infection. This is why we eat gluten-free today and why I put so much energy into utilizing real food for energy and nourishment. I'm a believer in using whole food as fuel and food as medicine. I know, it's corny, but hey, it works! Focusing on real food, gluten-free food and key nutrients has helped us heal and then thrive!

I shared tips and tricks of ours on my blog for years. During that time, I found myself becoming a "sherpa" gluten-free guide to others as well. Those looking for nutritional guidance and simple healthy gluten-free recipes. It's all making sense now, right?

Some of the most popular recipes on my blog have been power bowl recipes. Not just because the recipe itself is awesome (I may be biased), but also because the bowl recipe has a function and a purpose. Food always has a purpose, especially when it comes to fueling athletes.

These power bowls, nourish bowls, fuel bowls (or whatever you might call them), are a way for me to share the best synergy superfood recipes all in one pretty, rounded serving. They are easy to prep, easy to eat, easy to clean up and very portable. So basically, bowls full of key fuel and nourishment for us everyday folk, kids, athletes and all.

With each nourish bowl recipe, I do my best to explain how and why these foods can support you and your family's nutritional needs. Whether that is to energize, heal, recover, fuel or just happily feed your family!

I truly hope you enjoy these nourish bowls and know they have been created for you with LOVE. There I go again, being all corny. It's in my nature!

TIPS AND TRICKS FOR THE BOWLS

RICED OR SPIRALIZED VEGETABLES

You will notice that many of these nourish bowls use vegetables as a grain substitute; for instance, spiralized sweet potato spaghetti or cauliflower rice. This is a great way to boost nutrition while lowering carbohydrates and eliminating grains. When you prepare these riced vegetables and noodles, be sure to pat them dry with a paper towel as much as possible. This will remove excess water so they don't become soft or mushy later. It also helps keep them fresher, longer. Be sure to store them in an air-tight container in the fridge until you are ready to cook or eat.

Steaming spiralized vegetables is simple and can even be done in the microwave. Just place noodles in a microwave-safe bowl with a touch of water. Microwave on high for 1 minute, then check to see if the noodles are cooked to your liking, texture-wise. Repeat if necessary.

For crisper spiralized vegetables noodles, place on a baking sheet in the oven for about 15 to 20 minutes at 400 to 425°F (204 to 218°C), until soft enough to use as pasta.

If you don't have a spiralizer, feel free to cut the vegetables julienne style or use a peeler to create ribbon vegetable noodles. In doing so, you might need to buy extra vegetables so you can get the right amount of servings for each recipe. One spiralized zucchini will produce more noodles than one julienne or ribbon-cut zucchini. My personal favorite is the spiralizer, but you can work with what you have on hand!

GLUTEN-FREE GRAINS

Gluten-free grain options include gluten-free rolled oats, white rice, brown rice, quinoa, wild rice, black rice, jasmine rice and basmati.

One tool that has saved me lots of time in the kitchen is a rice cooker. All you do is set it and go! You can use a rice cooker to cook brown rice, white rice, quinoa, oats and more. Most rice cookers suggest following the standard stovetop directions. Be sure to verify before cooking.

OILS AND VINEGARS

I primarily use avocado oil, olive oil and coconut oil as my vegan or Paleo cooking oil. Avocado oil and coconut oil have a higher smoking point than most other vegetable oils, which helps preserve nutrients while cooking.

Both avocado oil and coconut oil work great in stir-fry, baking, etc. Be sure to look for 100% pure avocado oil and coconut oil. I often use naturally unrefined coconut oil for baking and cooking foods in high heat. It has less of a coconut taste and is odorless, which makes it a great fat to cook with. Naturally unrefined coconut oil does not have the same health benefits as virgin unrefined coconut oil, but it still is a great source of healthy fatty acids, such as medium-chain triglycerides (MCTs).

For olive oil, I prefer cold-pressed and extra virgin. For a Paleo option, feel free to use clarified butter or ghee when cooking at high heat, or simply use the virgin unrefined coconut oil.

My favorite cooking vinegars to use are tamari, rice wine vinegar, red wine vinegar, apple cider vinegar and white wine vinegar. You can use these in salad dressings as well. If you are looking for a stricter Paleo option, you can use coconut aminos in place of tamari. The Coconut Secret has a great line of gluten-free and vegan coconut products, including coconut aminos.

For most Asian dishes, chili sauce or Sriracha sauce can be used. San-j is a brand that I prefer that has gluten-free Asian sauces. Otherwise, please check the ingredients to make sure there is no added soy sauce or wheat.

HERBS AND SEASONINGS

I suggest using real fine sea salt or kosher salt. Both are minimally processed and have more minerals in them. Very fine pink Himalayan sea salt is my favorite sea salt and what I use for the majority of the recipes in this cookbook. It adds wonderful flavor and nutrients.

Some sea salt will lose its flavor during the cooking process. I recommend "to taste" during and after cooking to adjust to your liking. Everyone's palates are different, as well as their dietary restrictions.

I love using fresh herbs in my recipes! They help make each dish more flavorful, nourishing and bright! One of my favorite herbs is cilantro. I use fresh cilantro in most of my Spanish and Asian style nourish bowls. Cilantro is sometimes referred to as coriander leaves, Mexican parsley or Chinese parsley in the produce section. Make sure to use the fresh plant leaves, not the seed, unless otherwise specified.

If you are in a bind and don't have garlic cloves, you can use premade minced garlic or garlic powder. Just make sure it doesn't have any unfamiliar preservatives added. Two to three cloves of garlic equals roughly 1 teaspoon of minced garlic or ½ teaspoon of garlic powder.

SMOOTHIE BOWLS

The key to making a thick smoothie bowl is adding 1 or 2 servings of a frozen, starchy fruit or vegetable, such as banana or mango. You can also thicken smoothies by adding avocado, protein powder or frozen nut butter. Although frozen nut butter is a bit more difficult when processing it into a smoothie (you will need to blend very slowly and be patient), it does work! If you don't have a blender, a food processor will work as well.

DAIRY

Many of the recipes included in this book have a dairy topping. Please know that not all dairy is created equal. The best sources of dairy are organic cultured dairy or aged natural cheese. These will have fewer hormones and less lactose in them. I recommend using grass-fed yogurt, kefir yogurt, cultured sour cream or hard cheese topping if you choose to include dairy. You can find many of these in the dairy section at your local grocer. They may be a bit more expensive, but in the long run, they are better for your overall health.

VEGAN DAIRY

If you cannot tolerate dairy or are vegan, have no fear, there are still lots of options!

Nondairy milk or cream can include unsweetened almond milk, coconut milk and coconut cream. For Asian dishes and curries, it's best to use coconut milk and coconut cream found in the Asian aisle of your supermarket.

Instead of Parmesan, use nutritional yeast. Nutritional yeast is packed with B vitamins, iron and protein.

Instead of a cream sauce, make cashew cream or use chilled coconut cream. I use these substitutes in the Creamy Red Pepper Carrot Pappardelle Pasta Bowl (page 113), the Vanilla Cheesecake Bowls with Fruit (page 161) and the Blueberries 'n Cream Bowls (page 169).

There are several brands now making nondairy yogurt and sour cream. I prefer So Delicious and Silk. They have a variety of coconut, organic soy and even almond yogurts.

HEALTHY PROTEIN

Healthy protein choices include wild-caught salmon, canned wild-caught tuna (responsibly-caught), organic hormone-free chicken, beef, turkey and pork. For breakfast, look for uncured nitrate-free bacon and organic or free-range eggs.

Vegan protein options include chickpeas, cultured gluten-free tempeh, lentils and beans properly prepared or from a Bisphenol A (BPA)–free can.

For protein powder, I like to use a sprouted rice or pea protein. Sprouted proteins help you digest the nutrients better. Other healthy protein powders (non-vegan) include grass-fed whey protein, egg white protein and collagen protein powder.

UNREFINED SUGAR

Unrefined sugars (or types of sugar) skip the refining process and are more pure. Unrefined sugars and sweeteners include coconut palm sugar, molasses, honey, maple syrup, agave nectar, sucanat (whole cane sugar), fruit and date sugar. The crystalized unrefined sugars (such as coconut sugar) have a lighter, nuttier taste, which is why I use them in combination with liquid sugars, like honey or maple syrup.

If you don't have any of these sugars, I suggest checking out Wholesome Sweet Brand for options or the baking section at your local grocer. Most grocers carry some form of natural sweetener.

Most unrefined crystalized sugars can replace brown sugar 1:1.

ENERGIZING BREAKFAST BOWLS

Breakfast! It's the most important meal of the day, right? So often we forget just how important breakfast is: It literally means to break the fast. I'd like to add "and fuel up" to that. Breakfast doesn't have to be a hassle; it just needs to be filled with the right energizing nutrients! These energizing breakfasts are some of my favorite ways to utilize every nutrient you can. Whether it is a simple smoothie bowl, a quick oatmeal bowl or even a weekend brunch bowl, it's all good fuel for the day.

RASPBERRY SUNRISE BOWLS

These bowls are the perfect way to start the day! Gluten-free oats cooked with natural sugars act as carbohydrates and glycogen for fueling your muscles. The berries and orange give you a boost of vitamin C to protect your immune system so you can tackle the day. Easy, healthy and convenient! Make these the night before and wake up to a pre-made breakfast!

PREP TIME: 5 MINUTES • COOKING TIME: 20 MINUTES • SERVES: 2

BOWLS
1 cup (80 g) gluten-free rolled oats or quick oats
1 cup (240 ml) coconut or almond milk
Pinch of fine sea salt or kosher salt
1 tbsp (10 g) chia seeds
Vegan butter or almond butter, optional

FRUIT COMPOTE
¼ to ⅓ cup (60 to 75 ml) orange juice
1 tbsp (15 ml) coconut oil
1 to 2 tbsp (15 to 30 ml) maple syrup
Pinch of nutmeg
Pinch of ground ginger
¼ tsp cinnamon
1 cup (140 g) fresh berries

TOPPINGS
Sliced orange
Crushed nuts
Gluten-free granola, optional
2 oz (60 g) coconut cream or dairy-free yogurt, optional

In a microwave-safe bowl, microwave the gluten-free rolled oats, milk, salt and chia seeds for 2 to 3 minutes. For stovetop cooking, place the oats, milk, salt and chia in a small saucepan, then cook on medium heat for 10 minutes, or until the milk is absorbed. Add the optional vegan butter to make it creamier, if desired. Set aside.

To make the fruit compote, combine the orange juice, coconut oil and maple syrup in a small saucepan over low heat. Add the nutmeg, ginger, cinnamon and berries. Bring the mixture to a soft boil for 1 to 2 minutes. Reduce the heat and simmer for 10 minutes, until the fruit starts to soften. Mash the berries with a spoon to form a fruit compote.

Divide the oats into two bowls. Spoon the fruit compote over each bowl. Top with sliced oranges, nuts, granola and coconut cream, if desired.

CREAMY POLENTA BOWLS

These Italian style grits with sautéed veggies and egg will be another wholesome yet balanced breakfast to add to the menu. This is a nourishing meal that will definitely keep you full for hours! It also makes a great dinner if you want to switch things up.

PREP TIME: 10 MINUTES • COOKING TIME: 30 MINUTES • SERVES: 2 TO 3

3½ cups (828 ml) vegetable or chicken broth

1 tsp fine sea salt or kosher salt, plus more to taste

1 cup (170 g) uncooked stone ground polenta (see notes)

⅓ to ½ cup (80 to 120 ml) almond milk

1 tbsp (15 ml) avocado or olive oil, or clarified butter

Pinch of cumin

½ tsp curry

2½ cups (375 g) cherry tomatoes, divided

1 tsp minced garlic

2 tbsp (30 ml) olive oil, divided

Pepper, to taste

2 baby bok choy

1 cup (40 g) spinach leaves

2 to 3 eggs

TOPPINGS

1 green onion, green portion only

Crumbled feta or Parmesan shavings

Cooked nitrate-free bacon crumbles

1 tsp red pepper flakes

In a saucepan, bring the broth to a quick boil over medium-high heat. Add the salt and carefully pour the uncooked polenta into the boiling broth. Whisk gently, then pour in the almond milk, whisking again.

Turn the heat to low and continue stirring the polenta until it begins to thicken. Cook on low, covered, for about 25 to 30 minutes. Check the polenta every 10 minutes and stir to avoid clumps. After 25 minutes, add the oil, cumin, curry and ½ cup (80 g) of cherry tomatoes to the polenta. Cook on low for an additional 5 minutes.

Once the polenta is creamy and cooked, remove from the stove and place in a blender, or in a bowl with a hand mixer. Add the garlic, 1 tablespoon (15 ml) oil and a pinch of salt and pepper. Blend on medium until the tomatoes and seasonings are well combined.

Divide the polenta into two bowls and set aside while you cook the remaining ingredients.

Slice the bok choy in half lengthwise. Place the bok choy in a pan with the fresh spinach and remaining cherry tomatoes. Add 1 tablespoon (15 ml) of oil and sauté for 5 minutes, or until the vegetables are softened and cooked to your liking. Remove the vegetables from the pan, reserving the oil.

Add the two eggs to the same pan and fry on medium until the yolks are set, about 1 minute. Once the yolks are set, remove the pan from the heat. The outer egg's white portion should be slightly crispy.

Top each polenta bowl with half of the cooked vegetables and 1 egg. Garnish with the green onion, crumbled feta, crumbled bacon and a sprinkle of red pepper flakes.

Notes: Be sure to look for 100% stone ground cornmeal polenta.

The rice cooker is an easy way to cook polenta. You can simply place the ingredients listed to cook the polenta into your rice cooker and cook on the white rice setting until done. You may need to stir a few times while cooking.

Leftover polenta will solidify once you store it in the fridge. In order to make it creamy again, I like to warm a little broth or almond milk and stir it into the leftover polenta. It won't be as creamy as the first time you made it, but it's still delicious!

TROPICAL OVERNIGHT MUESLI BOWLS

Something a little new and refreshing for breakfast, these zesty Tropical Overnight Muesli Bowls are gluten-free, nutrient rich and energizing. The trick is to make this recipe the night before so you can get all those healthy digestion perks from soaking your oats, not to mention the easy meal prep!

PREP TIME: 10 MINUTES • COOKING TIME: 0 MINUTES • SERVES: 1 TO 2

GLUTEN-FREE MUESLI
1 cup (80 g) gluten-free rolled oats

2 tbsp (15 g) vanilla protein powder (see notes)

1 tbsp (10 g) chia seeds

¼ cup (45 g) raw almonds

2 tbsp (15 g) seed granola

TROPICAL YOGURT BLEND
1 banana

1 tbsp (15 ml) lime juice

8 oz (230 g) vanilla or coconut yogurt (see notes)

1 to 2 tsp (5 to 10 ml) coconut oil

Pinch of ginger or cinnamon

2 to 4 tbsp (30 to 60 ml) honey, optional

1 to 2 mint leaves, optional

TOPPINGS
1 to 2 tbsp (15 to 30 ml) coconut milk or almond milk

2 to 3 tbsp (15 to 25 g) gluten-free granola

Lime wedges

Lime zest

3 to 4 mint leaves

Toasted sesame seeds

Unsweetened coconut flakes, optional

To make the gluten-free muesli, combine the oats, protein powder, chia seeds, almonds and granola in a medium-size bowl. Set aside.

To make the tropical yogurt blend, combine the banana, lime juice, yogurt, coconut oil, spice, honey and mint in a blender. Blend until creamy and adjust sweetness if desired.

Pour the yogurt blend over the homemade muesli mix and let soak overnight or for at least a couple of hours.

After soaking the muesli in yogurt, serve in bowls or 1 large bowl. Top with the coconut milk, granola, lime wedges, lime zest, mint leaves, sesame seeds and coconut flakes, if desired.

Notes: You can substitute the protein powder with a bit of coconut flour mixed with vanilla extract, or omit from the recipe.

For a nutritional boost and more protein, feel free to substitute the yogurt with Greek yogurt.

NOURISHING SUPERFOOD BOWLS ✕ 20

PUMPKIN CHAI LATTE BOWLS

These Pumpkin Chai Latte Bowls are energy-packed to set your day off right. A fall-inspired recipe that is not only healthy and nourishing, but full of antioxidant-rich spices and immunity-boosting nutrients. This bowl is often my Monday breakfast! It's comforting yet energizing, and puts me in the best mood with all of the warming spices.

PREP TIME: 2 TO 24 HOURS • COOKING TIME: LESS THAN 3 MINUTES • SERVES: 2 TO 3

CHAI MIX
1 tsp cinnamon

½ tsp cardamom

¼ tsp ground cloves

½ tsp ground ginger

¼ tsp ground white or black pepper

Pinch of fine sea salt or kosher salt

BOWLS
10 oz (285 ml) almond milk or coconut drinking milk

2 to 3 tbsp (15 to 30 ml) maple syrup (see notes)

2 tbsp (23 g) pumpkin puree

1 cup (80 g) gluten-free rolled oats or quick oats

¾ to 1 cup (120 to 160 g) cooked gluten-free ancient grains (see notes)

1 tbsp (4 g) chia or flax seed

2 to 3 tbsp (14 to 20 g) slivered almonds or pumpkin seeds

1 tbsp (12 g) dark chocolate chips, optional

TOPPINGS
2 tbsp (30 g) yogurt (see notes)

1 tbsp (12 g) pumpkin puree, optional

Pumpkin spice

Dark chocolate almonds

Molasses

To make the chai mix, combine the cinnamon, cardamom, cloves, ginger, pepper and salt in a small bowl, mixing well. Set aside.

On the stovetop in a small saucepan, add the almond milk with the chai spices, maple syrup and pumpkin. Heat to medium-high and whisk until the spices are mixed in well and the syrup is dissolved. Remove from the heat.

In a large bowl, arrange the oats, ancient grains and chia seed. Pour 6 to 8 ounces (170 to 230 ml) of the pumpkin chai latte mix on top. Reserve the remaining pumpkin chai latte.

Place the bowl in the fridge for at least 2 hours or up to 24 hours overnight.

Once the oats have soaked, remove from the fridge. Scoop ½ to ⅔ cup (105 to 160 g) into serving bowls. Reheat if desired. Add the almonds and dark chocolate chips to each bowl if desired.

For the toppings, mix the yogurt with the pumpkin puree if desired and place on top of each bowl. Sprinkle with pumpkin spice, then add additional toppings.

The extra pumpkin chai latte is to enjoy heated, on its own. The additional latte can also be poured on the oats if they are too thick after soaking for a few hours.

Notes: For a quicker version or if you don't want to wait 2 hours, place the bowls in the microwave and heat for 1 to 2 minutes after pouring your latte mix on top. Then add the toppings.

For sweeter oats, drizzle each bowl with an extra tablespoon (15 ml) of maple syrup.

You can use vegan yogurt or omit the yogurt topping altogether for a dairy-free version.

Kasha (toasted buckwheat) and oats make a delicious combo for this recipe, but feel free to use other gluten-free grains such as quinoa, brown rice or millet. Another option is to use leftover cooked grains to save on time and prep.

HEALING GREEN SMOOTHIE BOWLS

What makes these smoothie bowls so healing? Well, lots actually! Kiwi, avocado, cinnamon and ginger are all healing for the stomach and soothing for digestion. A handful of spinach adds more vitamin C content as well as boosting immunity.

PREP TIME: 10 MINUTES • COOKING TIME: 0 MINUTES • SERVES: 2

2 frozen bananas

½ avocado, skin and pit removed (see notes)

1 kiwi, skin removed, plus extra slices for topping

2 slices peeled fresh ginger root, or 1 tsp ground ginger

2 cups (80 g) spinach leaves

1 tsp cinnamon

1 tbsp (12 g) tahini or creamy cashew butter

⅔ to ¾ cup (155 to 177 ml) coconut drinking milk (see notes)

1 to 2 tbsp (15 to 30 ml) maple syrup or honey, plus more for topping

2 tsp (7 g) green powder or spirulina

1 tbsp (10 g) flaxseed or chia seeds, for topping

Sliced strawberries, for topping

In a blender, combine the banana, avocado, kiwi, ginger, spinach, cinnamon, tahini, coconut milk and maple syrup. Blend until thick. You might have to stop a few times and scrape down the sides.

Once blended, add the green powder and blend again until mixed. Pour into two bowls. Top the bowls with the flaxseed, kiwi and strawberry slices. You can add extra maple syrup on top, if desired.

Notes: The avocado makes this bowl thick, like a combo of a pudding and a smoothie.

Be sure to use coconut drinking milk, rather than canned coconut milk. The less you add, the thicker the bowl will be.

VEGAN • PALEO

MANGO TANGO GLOW BOWLS

I love the turmeric glow you get from these smoothie bowls. The turmeric tea golden milk, combined with the fruit, provides mega anti-inflammatory boosting nutrients and is packed with a whole lot of nourishment! For a bonus, the pineapple juice is rich in the enzyme bromelain, which can help the body digest food and absorb nutrients more efficiently. Now that's how to mango tango with real food!

PREP TIME: 10 MINUTES • COOKING TIME: 10 MINUTES • SERVES: 1 TO 2

GOLDEN MILK
2 cups (480 ml) coconut milk, canned or drinking milk

1 tsp ground turmeric

Pinch of black pepper

½ tsp ground ginger

1 tbsp (15 ml) agave, maple syrup or honey

BOWL
1 frozen banana

2 cups (490 g) frozen pineapple

1 cup (95 g) frozen mango

1 tsp vanilla, or less to taste

Agave or maple syrup, optional

TOPPINGS
Grated ginger

Chia seeds

In a small saucepan or stockpot, brew the golden milk by combining the coconut milk, turmeric, black pepper, ginger and agave. Bring the milk to a soft boil, then reduce the heat to low and simmer for 5 minutes. Whisk until blended, then remove and let cool in the fridge.

In a blender, combine the golden milk, banana, pineapple, mango, vanilla and agave if desired. Blend until smooth.

Serve as one large bowl or two small bowls.

Top with the fresh grated ginger and chia seeds for crunch.

Note: These smoothie bowls are perfect for soothing those muscles post workout.

MEXICAN SAVORY OATMEAL BOWL

Don't knock it till you try it! Savory oats are a thing—a great thing! And this balanced breakfast bowl will prove it. Mexican spices, peppers, whole-grain gluten-free oats, salsa and an egg on top is the perfect balanced breakfast. This savory breakfast bowl is a great way to switch up your breakfast routine and start your day without a sugar rush.

PREP TIME: 10 MINUTES • COOKING TIME: 20 MINUTES • SERVES: 1

1 cup (240 ml) water

Pinch or more of sea salt or kosher salt

½ cup (40 g) gluten-free thick rolled oats (see note)

½ tsp cumin

Fine sea salt or kosher salt, to taste

Pepper, to taste

½ cup (80 g) thick salsa

2 tsp (10 ml) oil

1 egg

Fresh chopped cilantro

1 red pepper or red jalapeño, sliced

Sprinkle of grated cheese, optional

½ tbsp (7 ml) melted butter or dairy-free butter

In a small or medium pan, bring the water and salt to a boil. Add the oats, reduce the heat to medium-low and simmer for 15 to 20 minutes, or until thick, stirring occasionally. Remove the oats from the stove and mix in the cumin, salt and pepper.

Place the oats in a bowl with the salsa layered on top and set aside.

Heat a skillet with the oil over medium-high heat and fry the egg until the white is set, about 1 to 2 minutes. Place the fried egg on top of the oats and salsa.

Top with the cilantro, pepper and cheese, if desired. For added creaminess, drizzle the melted butter on top.

Note: You can also cook the oats in the microwave. In a large bowl, combine the ½ cup (40 g) of oats with 1½ cups (355 ml) of water. Cover and microwave on high for 3 to 4 minutes. Let stand for 2 minutes. Be sure to use a deep microwave-safe bowl so the water doesn't overflow.

MIDNIGHT MOCHA OATMEAL BOWLS

Have you had midnight mocha? It's basically dark chocolate, espresso and steamed milk. Well, I think it's better in oatmeal form and this bowl is why I wake up in the morning! Melted rich, dark chocolate mixed into an almond milk latte then poured into a wholesome bowl of gluten-free oats . . . Oh so decadent, yet satisfying. Vegan friendly, too!

PREP TIME: 10 MINUTES • COOKING TIME: 1 TO 10 MINUTES • SERVES: 2

½ to ⅓ cup (120 to 180 ml) brewed coffee

½ to ⅓ cup (120 to 180 ml) drinking coconut milk or almond milk, plus more for topping

1 cup (80 g) gluten-free rolled oats

⅓ cup (40 g) unsweetened cocoa powder, plus extra for topping

⅓ cup (60 g) dark chocolate chips, plus more for topping

½ cup (40 g) unsweetened coconut

¼ cup (40 g) black chia seed or flaxseed, plus more for topping

Maple syrup, optional

Mix the brewed coffee with the coconut milk. Pour ¼ cup (60 ml) of the coffee mixture over the oats in either a microwave-safe bowl or a saucepan on the stovetop. For the microwave, the oats and coffee should cook for about 1 to 2 minutes. On the stovetop over medium heat, the oats should cook for 5 to 10 minutes, or until the liquid is absorbed.

Keep an extra ¼ to ⅓ cup (60 to 80 ml) of the coffee mixture for topping. Once the oats are heated, add in the cocoa and stir together.

Divide the oats into two bowls. Add in the chocolate chips, coconut, chia and maple syrup, if desired.

Pour the rest of the coffee mixture on top and sprinkle with the cocoa powder. Feel free to add more coconut milk or cream to make the oats more creamy.

Top with additional dark chocolate and chia seeds.

MINT ALMOND MATCHA SMOOTHIE BOWL

Have you been too intimidated to try matcha, that green powder everyone raves about? Well, here's the perfect bowl recipe to give it a whirl! Matcha is packed with antioxidants, and a little matcha tea powder provides instant energy without leaving you feeling jittery. This bowl is the perfect powerhouse breakfast!

PREP TIME: 3 TO 4 HOURS • COOKING TIME: 0 MINUTES • SERVES: 1

1 cup (240 ml) almond milk

1 frozen banana, peeled and sliced

½ cup (120 ml) coconut drinking milk

1 tsp vanilla

1 tbsp (12 g) creamy natural almond butter

1 tsp matcha powder

Maple syrup, to taste

Avocado, optional

Vanilla protein powder, optional

3 mint leaves

1 to 2 tbsp (10 to 20 g) flaxseed or chia seed

Pour the almond milk into an ice cube tray and place in the freezer. At this time, also place the banana in the freezer. Freeze for 3 to 4 hours, or overnight until solid. Remove the ice cubes from the tray and the banana from the freezer, and set aside.

In a blender, combine the almond milk ice cubes, banana, coconut milk, vanilla, almond butter, matcha powder and maple syrup. Blend until smooth and thick. The frozen almond milk might take some time, so be patient and stop the blender to give it a rest when blending.

For a thicker smoothie bowl, you can add ½ an avocado or 1 scoop of vanilla protein powder to the blender and simply blend again.

Top with fresh mint leaves and flaxseeds.

ANTI-INFLAMMATORY SUPERFOOD SMOOTHIE BOWLS

If the body is chronically stressed, real food can do wonders to repair it. Yes, this is one serious smoothie bowl. Beets, purple cabbage, cherry juice and pineapple contains properties to reduce inflammation in the body. Perfect for a post- workout snack/meal or even post travel!

PREP TIME: 3 TO 4 HOURS • COOKING TIME: 0 MINUTES • SERVES: 1 TO 2

1 small frozen banana

½ to 1 cup (170 to 340 g) purple cabbage or purple carrot (see note)

1 cup (240 ml) tart cherry or pineapple juice

½ cup (70 g) peeled beets (cooked or raw)

2 to 3 tsp (10 to 15 g) fresh ginger or ¼ tsp ground

3 tbsp (45 ml) maple syrup

1 tsp vanilla extract, optional

1 tbsp (10 g) chia seeds for bowl, plus more for topping

Chilled coconut drinking milk or canned cream, for topping

Place the banana in the freezer. Freeze for 3 to 4 hours, or until solid. Remove the banana from the freezer, and set aside.

In a blender, combine the banana, cabbage, cherry juice, beets, ginger, maple syrup, vanilla and chia seeds. Blend until creamy, and pour into serving bowls or 1 large bowl.

Drizzle the chilled coconut milk on top, and add extra chia seeds for topping.

Note: The cabbage taste is disguised in the smoothie due to the other delicious fruits and add-ins. That being said, feel free to omit if you prefer just fruit.

PURPLE POWER SMOOTHIE BOWLS

Creamy and fruity, these Purple Power Smoothie Bowls are packed with purple superfood ingredients to boost energy, stamina and vitality. Don't be scared—you can't even taste the secret veggies added! The blue, black and red berries make it sweet, and the banana helps make this smoothie bowl extra creamy. Just add a scoop of flavored protein powder and you've got yourself a well-balanced meal in a bowl.

PREP TIME: 10 MINUTES • COOKING TIME: 0 MINUTES • SERVES: 2

1 cup (150 g) beets, peeled and diced (see note)

1 cup (150 g) frozen blueberries

1 cup (125 g) frozen raspberries, plus more for topping

½ cup (75 g) blackberries

1 cup (240 ml) almond milk

½ large banana, fresh or frozen

1 tbsp (15 ml) maple syrup

½ avocado, skin and pit removed

2 oz (60 g) protein powder of choice, chocolate or vanilla, optional

TOPPINGS
Cocoa powder

Handful of slivered almonds

Splash of coconut drinking milk

Rolled oats, optional

Unsweetened shredded coconut, optional

In a blender, place the beets, blueberries, raspberries, blackberries, almond milk, banana, maple syrup and avocado, and blend until smooth.

For an extra thick smoothie bowl and for additional protein, add a scoop of protein powder, and blend again.

Pour into 2 bowls. Top with cocoa powder, almonds, coconut milk, rolled oats and shredded coconut, if desired.

Note: In this smoothie bowl, you can use raw or cooked beets. For a creamier bowl, I recommend using cooked beets.

STRAWBERRY PB SWIRL SMOOTHIE BOWLS

When I was in college, I used to freeze peanut butter in ice trays for a dessert. I often would put a spoonful of jelly in the middle too . . . I know, so strange. But also, so GENIUS! Freezing natural peanut butter is what makes these bowls extra thick and creamy. But don't forget to add nature's candy, aka strawberries! Healthy fats, rich in vitamin C, fiber and dairy-free.

PREP TIME: 3 TO 4 HOURS • COOKING TIME: 30 SECONDS • SERVES: 1 TO 2

2 tbsp (25 g) frozen almond or peanut butter

1 cup (240 ml) almond milk, divided

1 cup (150 g) frozen strawberries

1 small banana

Pinch of ginger

¼ tsp cinnamon

1 tbsp (15 ml) honey or maple syrup

½ kiwi or mango, for extra tartness, optional

1 tbsp (12 g) almond or peanut butter

1 tsp coconut oil or butter

TOPPINGS
Almond slivers

Gluten-free oats or granola

Flaxseed

Maple syrup

Scoop the almond butter into an ice cube tray and place in the freezer. Freeze for 3 to 4 hours, or until solid. Remove the ice cubes from the tray, and set aside.

In a blender, add the frozen nut butter and 2 tablespoons (30 ml) of the almond milk. Blend until smooth. Be patient as this could take a while, but the frozen nut butter will eventually get creamy and thick. It's the perfect thickener for smoothie bowls.

Add the remaining almond milk, strawberries, banana, ginger, cinnamon, honey and kiwi, if desired. Blend until smooth and pour into serving bowls.

In a small microwave-safe bowl, add the nut butter and coconut oil, and melt in the microwave for 30 seconds or less. Whisk together and drizzle over each bowl or 1 large bowl. Top the bowls with almond slivers, gluten-free oats, flaxseed and maple syrup.

Note: For the Paleo option, use almond butter in place of peanut butter.

COUNTRY VEGETABLE SCRAMBLE BOWLS

Good ol' country scramble. We are using only fresh, real food ingredients here: eggs, potatoes, uncured bacon and seasonal vegetables fresh from the farm! One of my favorite real food bowls that cooks up in a jiffy! Great for brunch or fueling up for a big day.

PREP TIME: 10 MINUTES • COOKING TIME: 20 MINUTES • SERVES: 2

3 new potatoes

¼ cup (60 ml) water

1 large broccoli stem or ½ cup (45 g) chopped broccoli as alternative

2 large carrots

1 to 2 large eggs

1 to 2 tbsp (15 to 30 ml) almond or coconut milk

½ to 1 tbsp (8 to 15 g) butter or olive oil

3 to 4 slices uncured bacon, chopped

½ tsp garlic, minced

½ cup (80 g) cherry tomatoes, sliced or diced

¼ tsp cumin

Pinch of paprika

¼ tsp fine sea salt

Black pepper, to taste

4 large asparagus spears, shaved (see notes)

1 green onion, green portion only, chopped, for garnish

Shaved Parmesan, for garnish

Herbs, for garnish

Slice the new potatoes into quarters, about ⅓-inch (8-mm) thick. Place in a saucepan with the water. Cover and lightly steam for 3 to 4 minutes or until the potatoes are softened. Remove from the heat and discard the excess water.

Spiralize or julienne the broccoli stem and carrots. Place in a bowl and set aside.

Whisk together the eggs and milk in another bowl.

In a large skillet over medium heat, heat a pat of butter or oil. Place the bacon and steamed potatoes in the pan. Fry for 2 to 4 minutes, flipping once until the bacon starts to become brown and cooked on the outside. Spoon out any excess bacon grease from the pan, reserving a couple of tablespoons (30 ml) for cooking or coating vegetables. Then add the garlic, egg and milk mixture. Stir together.

Add the broccoli, carrots, tomatoes, cumin, paprika, salt and pepper to the pan, and stir-fry on medium to medium-high heat. Cook until the eggs are scrambled and the vegetables are lightly cooked, about 4 to 5 minutes. Add the asparagus shavings in the last minute, since they cook fast.

Divide into 2 bowls, and add the chopped green onion, Parmesan and herbs to garnish. Season with more salt and pepper to taste, if desired.

Notes: To make asparagus ribbons/shavings, use a julienne slicer or peeler and shave a large raw asparagus, starting with the stem and moving toward the spear.

For a Whole30 and Paleo option, omit the cheese and be sure to use clarified butter.

BLUEBERRY COCONUT RICE PORRIDGE BOWLS

This is one cozy yet refreshing breakfast bowl! It's easy to digest and packed with antioxidants and healthy plant-based fats. One of my go-to breakfast bowls for quick energy or even replenishing the body post workout.

PREP TIME: 5 MINUTES • COOKING TIME: 20 MINUTES • SERVES: 2 TO 3

1 to 1½ cups (210 to 315 g) rice (white, jasmine or basmati)

1½ cups (355 ml) water

½ to ⅔ cup (123 to 160 g) coconut milk, plus more for topping

1 cup (150 g) blueberries

2 tsp (10 ml) maple syrup

1 kiwi, sliced for topping

1 to 2 tbsp (10 to 20 g) chia seeds

In a medium-size saucepan, combine the rice, water and coconut milk over high heat and bring to a quick boil.

Cover and reduce the heat to a low simmer. Cook for an additional 15 minutes or until the rice is tender. Remove from the heat, cover and let sit for 10 minutes. When the liquid is absorbed, fluff with a fork and scoop into bowls.

Add the blueberries to each bowl. Heat the bowls for 1 minute in the microwave, covered, to soften the berries.

Remove from the microwave and add the maple syrup, kiwi slices, chia seeds and a dollop of coconut milk to each bowl.

Note: For easy prep, use a rice cooker with the same ratio of rice, water and coconut milk.

CURRIED LENTIL BOWLS

Curried lentils with your favorite protein make these the ideal recovery or balance bowls. The lentils in this bowl are the perfect balance of fats, carbohydrates and protein. Top them with iron-rich protein and veggies, plus anti-inflammatory spices, and you've got yourself the perfect bowl to nourish your body. This is an easy meal that will keep you full and refueled after a hard workout or long day!

PREP TIME: 5 MINUTES • COOKING TIME: 30 MINUTES • SERVES: 2 TO 3

1 cup (200 g) dry red, black or green lentils

¾ cup (177 ml) water

2¼ cups (530 ml) broth

½ tsp fine sea salt or kosher salt, plus more to taste

¼ cup (40 g) green onion, white portion, or white onion

1 tsp minced garlic

1 tbsp (15 ml) olive or avocado oil

4 oz (115 g) chopped chicken or pork, gluten-free sausage or cooked sausage

2 eggs

2 tbsp (30 ml) almond or coconut milk

¼ to ⅓ cup (60 to 80 ml) tomato sauce

¼ tsp or more curry powder

½ tsp smoked paprika

½ tsp black pepper

Pinch of cumin

3 cups (120 g) leafy greens

TOPPINGS

Sprinkle of crumbled goat cheese or other natural cheese

Red pepper flakes

Fresh cilantro or herb of choice

Sour cream or plain Greek yogurt

Balsamic vinegar, optional

Olive oil, optional

Rinse the lentils with water before boiling to remove any debris. In a large stockpot, add the lentils, water and broth. Bring to a boil, then cover and reduce the heat to a simmer until tender, around 15 to 20 minutes. Season the lentils with salt after cooking so they don't become tough.

Drain the extra liquid from the lentils once cooked, if needed. Set aside.

In a large skillet, cook the green onion and minced garlic in the oil for 2 minutes over medium heat. Add the chopped chicken. If using uncooked meat, brown halfway through or more, until pinkness disappears.

In a small bowl, whisk the eggs and milk and add to the skillet along with the cooked lentils, tomato sauce, curry powder, paprika, salt, black pepper and cumin.

Mix all of the ingredients together in the skillet and cook over medium heat until the eggs and meat are cooked through, about 4 to 5 minutes.

Steam the greens in a stockpot for 3 to 5 minutes until wilted, or microwave for 1 minute on high. Divide the steamed greens between the bowls. Top with 1 cup (200 g) of cooked lentils, cheese, red pepper flakes and cilantro. Add a dollop of sour cream and drizzle of balsamic vinegar and olive oil, if desired.

WEEKEND BRUNCH BOWLS

I have a major love of brunch food. But not just one thing, ALL THE THINGS! Eggs, toast with homemade preserves, pancakes, fruit and bacon—all on one plate, please! These brunch bowls are my way of slowing down and savoring on the weekend, not to mention filling up with wholesome food for hours.

PREP TIME: 40 MINUTES • COOKING TIME: 30 MINUTES • SERVES: 2 TO 3

FLOURLESS PANCAKES
2 eggs
1 large, ripe banana
4 oz (115 g) vanilla yogurt or plain yogurt
½ to ⅔ cup (75 to 100 g) tapioca starch or ground rolled oats
1 tsp baking powder
1 tsp cinnamon
Pinch of nutmeg, optional
1 tsp vanilla
¼ tsp fine sea salt or kosher salt
Coconut or avocado oil, or clarified butter, for cooking

SCRAMBLED EGGS
4 eggs
⅓ cup (80 ml) unsweetened coconut or almond milk
Dash of sea salt

BOWLS
½ cup (75 g) blueberries
1 cup (150 g) strawberries
1 orange, sliced
Maple syrup
Parsley or mint, for garnish

To make the flourless pancakes, place the eggs, banana and yogurt in a blender. Blend until creamy.

Add in the starch, baking powder, spices, vanilla and salt. Blend again until smooth. For thicker pancakes, add more starch 1 tablespoon (10 g) at a time. For crêpe-like pancakes, use ½ cup (75 g) of starch. Place the batter in the fridge for 30 minutes, and remove once the batter has thickened a bit.

Heat a skillet to medium-high, and add a few teaspoons of oil to coat the pan. Once hot, pour ⅓ cup (80 ml) of batter in the center of the pan. The batter will be a little thinner than normal pancake batter, but easy to flip.

Cook until the edges start to brown or the middle starts to bubble, usually no more than 2 minutes. Flip it over and let the pancake cook another 1 to 3 minutes. Remove the pancake and place it on the plate. Repeat. Yield will be 5 to 7 pancakes.

To make the eggs, whisk the eggs with the coconut milk and salt and scramble over medium heat for 1 to 2 minutes until eggs are softly set. Remove from the heat and set aside.

To assemble the bowls, add 2 to 3 pancakes per bowl. Divide the scrambled eggs, berries, strawberries and orange evenly among the bowls. Drizzle with maple syrup and garnish with parsley or mint.

Notes: The flourless pancakes are quick to make and also freeze well. For cooking the pancakes, cooking times will vary per pan. I recommended adding a little oil after making 1 to 2 pancakes. You can use a large skillet to cook multiple pancakes at once, but just be sure to keep an eye on them, as they can cook quickly.

If you are in a bind, you can use store-bought gluten-free pancakes or waffles. Van's has gluten-free options for both that are located in the freezer section.

ZIPPY LUNCH BOWLS

Zippy: My favorite word! It means quick, lively, refreshing and tasty! Okay, I added that last meaning, but I think you will agree that these zippy lunch bowls are quite tasty. These bowl recipes are ones you can make ahead for easy meal prep with minimal ingredients. But don't be fooled: Although these bowls may be simple and quick to make, they are still loaded with flavor and key vitamins and minerals to power you through the rest of the day.

HONEY-MISO SUMMER SALAD BOWLS

Sweet, tangy, crisp and refreshing; it's summer in a bowl. This salad has so many layers of flavors, it will make your tastebuds sing! One of my favorite components of this salad is the miso. Miso paste is made from fermented soybeans, which contains live lactobacilli. Those good bacteria can help our bodies absorb more nutrients. Just another great superfood we're adding to this super summer salad!

PREP TIME: 10 MINUTES • COOKING TIME: 3 TO 4 MINUTES • SERVES: 2

BOWLS

3 cups (120 g) spinach leaves

1 medium zucchini, shaved into thin slices (see notes)

1 cup (40 g) broccoli or alfalfa sprouts

½ cup (60 g) radishes, thinly sliced

1 cup (150 g) strawberries, sliced

Lemon slices, for garnish

Fresh basil, for garnish

Black sesame seeds or toasted sesame seeds, for topping

Salt, to taste

Cracked black pepper, to taste

HONEY-MISO DRESSING

3 tbsp (45 g) white miso paste (see notes)

3 tbsp (45 ml) sesame oil

1 tsp mustard

¼ cup (60 ml) honey or agave (see notes)

3 tbsp (45 ml) rice wine vinegar or red wine vinegar

1 tbsp (15 ml) lemon juice

Place a steam basket in a medium pot and add an inch (2.5 cm) of water. Place the spinach in the steamer, cover, bring to a boil and lightly steam the spinach leaves for 3 to 4 minutes. Another quick steam option is to place the spinach in the microwave for 30 to 45 seconds on high.

In two serving bowls, arrange the steamed spinach, zucchini, broccoli sprouts, radishes and strawberries.

To make the dressing, whisk together the white miso paste, sesame oil, mustard, agave, rice vinegar and lemon juice. Drizzle 1 to 2 tablespoons (15 to 30 ml) of the dressing on top of each bowl. Save the extra dressing for later use. It keeps in the fridge for up to 5 days.

Add the lemon slices, fresh basil and sesame seeds for garnish, and season with salt and pepper to taste.

Notes: A julienne slicer or peeler will work to shave the zucchini into flat noodles. Roll up the noodles before placing in each bowl.

This dish is naturally salty due to the miso, but feel free to add a pinch of sea salt if desired.

Is miso paste Paleo? Yes and no. Miso, being a fermented form of soy, can be used in many Paleo friendly recipes and has many health benefits. Be sure to check you are using the purest, gluten-free form.

For a vegan option, substitute agave for the honey in the dressing.

SEAFOOD ANTIPASTO SALAD BOWLS

When traveling in Italy, I loved slow dinners that were filled with multiple courses. The antipasto platter was my favorite! But I must say, all of the cured meats left me feeling a little blah. This Seafood Antipasto Salad Bowl is a lighter, low-carb version. Plus, it's hearty, healthy and packed with omega-3 fatty acids.

PREP TIME: 10 MINUTES • COOKING TIME: 0 MINUTES • SERVES: 2 TO 3

DRESSING
¼ tsp dried oregano
½ tsp ground pepper
¼ cup (60 ml) olive oil
2 to 3 tbsp (30 to 45 ml) red wine vinegar
Pinch of sea salt

BOWLS
3 to 4 oz (85 to 115 g) smoked salmon
1 apricot, sliced
1 radicchio head, chopped
1 cup (170 g) artichoke hearts, drained and sliced
½ cup (90 g) olives
2 cups (80 g) mixed leafy greens
2 oz (60 g) smoked or roasted salted almonds
2 tbsp (12 g) capers
1 to 2 oz (30 to 60 g) mozzarella or goat cheese crumbles
½ cup (80 g) cherry tomatoes, diced
⅓ cucumber, sliced
Fresh lemon juice
Parsley or fresh oregano sprigs, for garnish
Sea salt, to taste
Black pepper, to taste

To make the dressing, whisk together the ground oregano, pepper, olive oil, red wine vinegar and salt in a small bowl.

In a large bowl, add the smoked salmon, apricot, radicchio, artichoke hearts, olives, leafy greens, almonds, capers, mozzarella, cherry tomatoes and cucumber. Add the dressing and toss all of the ingredients to coat. Squeeze the fresh lemon juice over the salad.

Divide into 2 to 3 bowls. Garnish with the parsley or fresh oregano. Add fine sea salt and pepper to taste.

SAUCY FORBIDDEN RICE BOWLS

Don't worry, you're not forbidden from devouring these rice bowls. Forbidden rice, or black rice, is an ancient grain that has even more health perks than other rice varieties. It's rich in antioxidants, dietary fiber and protein, and has anti-inflammatory properties. Enjoy a bowl (or two) with steamed veggies and homemade almond sauce, and feel good about lunch.

PREP TIME: 10 MINUTES • COOKING TIME: 6 MINUTES • SERVES: 2

ALMOND SAUCE

1 tbsp (15 ml) almond butter, melted

½ cup (120 ml) sesame oil

½ tsp garlic, minced

1 tbsp (15 ml) Sriracha

½ to 1 tbsp (8 to 15 ml) lemon juice

2 tbsp (30 ml) rice vinegar

2 tsp (10 ml) tamari

Pinch of black or white pepper, to taste

1 tbsp (15 ml) agave or honey

Pinch of sea salt, optional

BOWLS

6 oz (170 g) cooked gluten-free tempeh (see notes)

1 small baby bok choy

1⅓ cups (220 g) cooked black rice (see notes)

1 cup (120 g) radishes, sliced

1 green apple, spiralized or julienne cut

1 green onion, chopped, for topping

Sesame seeds, for topping

Salted nori sheets or seaweed chips, for topping

Sprouts or fresh cilantro, for garnish

To make the almond sauce, whisk together the almond butter, sesame oil, garlic, Sriracha, lemon juice, rice vinegar, tamari, pepper, agave and salt in a small bowl. Taste and see if it's to your liking. Adjust the agave, pepper and salt if needed.

Coat the tempeh in half the sauce. Save the other half for drizzling on top.

Place a steam basket in a medium pot and add an inch (2.5 cm) of water. Add the bok choy in the steamer, cover, bring to a boil and lightly steam for 6 minutes. Slice in half.

In each bowl, evenly arrange the tempeh, bok choy, black rice, radishes and apple. Top with green onions, sesame seeds, nori sheets and cilantro. Drizzle extra sauce on top.

Notes: You can substitute the tempeh with other protein sources such as cooked chickpeas, wild-caught tuna (canned, drained), organic tuna or crab (canned, drained), or peeled cooked shrimp.

You can use brown or wild rice if you don't have black rice.

POWER BISTRO SALAD BOWLS

This Power Bistro Salad Bowl has all you need to satisfy your hunger without sacrificing taste. A hearty but healthy warm green salad, packed full of omega-rich seafood, choline (aka, the brain-power vitamin) from the eggs and healthy fats. Grain-free, full of fiber and low in sugar, it's the perfect power lunch bowl!

PREP TIME: 10 MINUTES • COOKING TIME: 10 MINUTES • SERVES: 2

½ to ¾ cup (80 to 120 g) cherry tomatoes, halved

1 to 2 tbsp (15 to 30 ml) olive oil, divided

⅛ tsp herbs de Provence

Fine sea salt, to taste

Pepper, to taste

¼ cup (40 g) diced onion or 4 pearl onions sliced in half

4 cups (160 g) chopped kale, spinach or any other leafy green

1 tsp water or broth

2 soft- or hard-boiled eggs

4 pieces or 4 oz (115 g) sliced peppered smoked salmon

¼ cup (30 g) feta, crumbled or cubed, plus more for topping

Handful of radishes, stems removed

Microgreens or sprouts

Balsamic vinegar

Olive oil

Roasted almonds or pine nuts, for topping

2 lemon wedges

Olives, optional

2 tbsp (20 g) dried fruit, chopped (Turkish figs, apricots or dates work great)

Garlic salt, optional

Preheat the oven to broil. Line a baking sheet with parchment paper.

In a small bowl, toss the cherry tomato halves with 1 teaspoon oil, herbs de Provence and a pinch of salt and pepper. Add the onions and spread the mixture on the prepared baking sheet and broil until the tomatoes are soft, about 5 minutes.

Place the kale in a small pot with the rest of the olive oil and a pinch of sea salt, pepper and the water. Cook over medium heat until the kale has wilted, about 2 to 4 minutes. Remove from the stove and set aside.

Divide the cooked kale and cherry tomato mixture equally into 2 bowls, sectioning them into different sides of the bowl. Add the egg, salmon, feta, radishes and microgreens to each bowl.

Drizzle the balsamic vinegar and olive oil over each bowl. Top each bowl with the crumbled feta, roasted almonds, lemon wedges, olives and dried fruit. Season with ground pepper to taste, and a pinch of garlic or sea salt, if desired.

KICKIN' ORANGE CHICKEN AND BROCCOLI RICE BOWLS

Orange chicken and rice is one of the most popular take-out foods. It sure is delicious! But it's usually not the healthiest, nor is it usually gluten-free. The problem is solved with this "healthified" version. Real orange and kickin' chili sauce makes for a tasty chicken marinade. Plus, you get a serving of extra veggies with the broccoli rice!

PREP TIME: 20 MINUTES • COOKING TIME: 30 MINUTES • SERVES: 4

MARINADE

⅓ cup (60 g) peeled mandarin orange slices, plus more slices for topping

2 tbsp (30 ml) chili sauce or Sriracha

1 tbsp (15 ml) lime juice

2 to 3 tbsp (30 to 45 ml) orange marmalade

¼ tsp fine sea salt or kosher salt, plus more to taste

¼ tsp black pepper, plus more to taste

1 tsp minced garlic

¼ cup (40 g) chopped red onion or shallot, plus more for topping

2 to 3 tbsp (15 to 30 ml) rice wine vinegar or dry white wine

¼ cup (60 ml) olive oil or avocado oil

2 to 3 tbsp (15 to 30 ml) gluten-free tamari

12 to 16 oz (340 to 455 g) skinless chicken breasts

BROCCOLI RICE

1 lb (454 g) broccoli florets, blended in food processor

2 to 3 tsp (10 to 15 ml) sesame oil

1 tbsp (10 g) sesame seeds

TOPPINGS

Lime slices

Crushed red chili pepper flakes

Cilantro

Tamari

To make the marinade, blend the orange slices, chili sauce, lime juice, orange marmalade, salt, pepper, garlic, red onion and rice wine vinegar in a food processor or blender until thoroughly mixed. Add the olive oil and tamari and blend again until creamy.

Place the chicken breasts in a single layer in a casserole dish and pour the marinade over the chicken. Place the dish in the fridge and marinate 20 minutes or longer.

Preheat the oven or grill to 425°F (218°C). Bake the chicken for 20 to 25 minutes. Set the oven to broil for the last minute of cooking.

For grilling, use a foil pack to cook the chicken. Grilling will take less time, so check for doneness at 15 minutes.

To make the broccoli rice, steam the blended broccoli in a microwave-safe bowl with sesame oil for 45 seconds. Add the sesame seeds to the rice, and salt and pepper to taste.

Equally divide the broccoli rice among the bowls, then add the chicken. Garnish with the orange slices, lime slices, red chili pepper flakes and cilantro. Drizzle on extra tamari or use for dipping.

GARLICKY PEA PESTO VEGGIE NOODLE BOWLS

Peas are so underrated, in my opinion. Those little seeds can do wonders to a dish, for instance, make pesto! This is one veggie-packed veggie noodles bowl made in a jiffy. No cooking required, it's filling and flavorful.

PREP TIME: 10 MINUTES • COOKING TIME: 0 MINUTES • SERVES: 1 TO 2

PESTO

1 cup (150 g) peas, fresh or thawed if frozen (see notes)

1 cup (120 g) raw walnut halves

½ to ⅔ cup (20 to 30 g) basil leaves

¼ tsp fine sea salt or kosher salt

Pinch of black pepper

½ lemon, juiced

3 cloves garlic

1 green onion, white and green parts only

⅓ cup (80 ml) olive oil, plus more for topping

BOWLS

2 summer squash, spiralized (see notes)

Garlic salt or powder

1 to 2 tbsp (7 to 15 g) crushed walnuts

Red pepper flakes

½ lemon, sliced

Dollop of sour cream or yogurt, optional

Microgreens or sprouts

In a food processor, blend the peas, walnuts, basil, salt, pepper, lemon juice, garlic and green onion until smooth, 3 to 5 minutes. Scrape the sides and add the oil after blending. Blend again until smooth.

For the noodles, press summer squash noodles with paper towel to remove excess water. Toss the noodles in a bowl with ⅓ to ½ cup (80 to 120 g) pea pesto. Usually ⅓ cup (80 g) is enough.

Add a pinch of garlic salt or garlic powder.

Serve in 2 small bowls or 1 large bowl. Top each bowl with the crushed walnuts, red pepper flakes, sliced lemon and salt and pepper to taste. Add the sour cream if desired.

Drizzle with olive oil and garnish with the microgreens.

Notes: Green peas have fewer phytates and toxins than other legumes. Some Paleo diets will allow them. For a more strict Paleo option, please use snap peas without the pod.

For the squash, julienne slice or make ribbons if you don't have a spiralizer.

GREEN GODDESS POWER SALAD BOWLS

Quick and easy, these Green Goddess Power Salad Bowls are nourishing, plant-based bowls packed with super greens, healthy fats and nature's candy and topped with homemade green goddess dressing. They will fill you up and nourish you all at once.

PREP TIME: 10 MINUTES • COOKING TIME: 0 MINUTES • SERVES: 2 TO 3

GREEN GODDESS DRESSING

⅓ cup (60 g) tahini or creamy cashew butter

1 tbsp (3 g) parsley, chopped

½ cup (25 g) green onion or red onion

1 tbsp (10 g) sesame seeds

2 tbsp (30 ml) gluten-free soy sauce or tamari

2 tbsp (30 ml) apple cider vinegar

2 tbsp (30 ml) lemon juice, about ½ of a lemon squeezed

1 tsp minced garlic or 2 cloves garlic

¼ to ½ tsp fine sea salt or kosher salt, to taste

Black pepper, to taste

⅓ cup (80 ml) coconut milk or unsweetened almond milk (see note)

¼ cup (60 ml) olive or avocado oil

BOWLS

5 to 6 cups (200 to 240 g) large-leaf spinach

⅓ to ½ cup (115 to 170 g) red or green cabbage, shaved

1 cup (40 g) microgreens or sprouts

¾ cup (30 g) fresh parsley

1 green apple, spiralized or thinly sliced

¾ to 1 cup (135 to 180 g) California Mission Figs, halved

2 to 3 tbsp (20 to 30 g) almonds and/or seeds

TOPPINGS

Fresh lemon slices

Fresh berries

Balsamic vinegar, optional

To make the green goddess dressing, place the tahini, parsley, green onion, sesame seeds, soy sauce, vinegar, lemon juice, garlic, salt, pepper and coconut milk in a food processor. Pulse a few times, then keep the food processor running and slowly add the oil. Add more salt to taste. Blend until creamy.

To make the bowls, arrange the spinach and cabbage in the bowls, depending on the desired salad size.

Divide the microgreens, parsley and apple, then arrange them around the spinach and cabbage in each bowl. Add 2 to 3 figs per bowl, then divide the almonds equally among the bowls.

Drizzle each bowl with the dressing, and garnish with the sliced lemon, berries and balsamic vinegar, if desired. Add salt and pepper to taste.

Note: Coconut milk in a can is fine to use, but will produce a thicker dressing. Coconut drinking milk or almond milk doesn't thicken as much in the fridge. If using canned coconut milk, add 2 tablespoons (30 ml) of water or oil to thin it out. For a thicker dressing, add in ⅓ of a ripe avocado.

5-MINUTE CHEESY ZUCCHETTI BOWL

Got 5 minutes? Then you've got one tasty homemade lunch! Zoodles mixed with a "cheesy" sauce make for one satisfying plant-based meal. Nutritional yeast is packed with B vitamins, which are key for those on a vegetarian or vegan diet.

PREP TIME: 5 MINUTES • COOKING TIME: 30 TO 45 SECONDS • SERVES: 1

2 small zucchinis

⅓ cup (50 g) nutritional yeast

¼ cup (60 ml) almond milk

1 to 2 tbsp (15 to 30 ml) olive oil

¼ tsp minced garlic

Sea salt or kosher salt, to taste

Pepper, to taste

2 tbsp (30 g) tomato sauce

1 plum tomato, sliced thin

Pinch of Italian seasoning

Fresh basil or parsley

Crushed red pepper flakes

1 tbsp (6 g) capers

Spiralize or julienne-cut the zucchini. Place in a bowl and press with a paper towel to remove the excess water. Drain the excess water from the bowl.

In a microwave-safe bowl, combine the nutritional yeast, almond milk, olive oil and garlic. Cook in the microwave for 30 to 45 seconds until warm. Remove and whisk the mixture until well combined. Add the salt, pepper and tomato sauce, and whisk again.

Toss the almond milk mixture with the zucchini noodles and add the sliced tomato. Add a sprinkle of Italian seasoning, basil, red pepper flakes and capers. Season with salt and pepper to taste, if desired.

Note: For an extra protein boost, add chickpeas, or chicken or gluten-free sausage, for a Paleo option.

SPRING PEA NOODLE BOWLS

Spring peas are truly the first sign of spring harvest! I love using fresh spring peas in a cold noodle salad. They make the perfect crunch to go along with that noodle slurp. These bowls take no time to make and are deliciously healthy. Spring peas contain quality protein, and generous amounts of vitamin B1 and folate.

PREP TIME: 20 MINUTES • COOKING TIME: 2 MINUTES • SERVES: 1 TO 2

2 oz (60 g) Asian rice noodles (see note)

3 cups (120 g) leafy greens, lightly steamed, if desired

Handful of spring snap peas, sliced open

1 cup (340 g) or more shaved veggies; cucumber, zucchini, carrots

1 cup (40 g) or more microgreens or sprouts

½ small shallot, sliced

Handful of pumpkin seeds, sesame seeds or crushed nuts

Sesame or olive oil, for topping

Rice wine or red wine vinegar, optional, for topping

Fresh lemon slices

Handful of fresh chopped cilantro

Fine sea salt or kosher salt, to taste

Pepper, to taste

Soak the Asian rice noodles for 20 minutes in hot water, then rinse with cold water. If the noodles are still not soft after soaking, place them in a pot of boiling water for 1 to 2 minutes, then drain and rinse in cold water.

Arrange in 1 to 2 bowls.

Divide the leafy greens, spring snap peas, shaved veggies, microgreens, shallot and pumpkin seeds equally between the 2 bowls or 1 large bowl, arranging around the noodles in each bowl. Top each bowl with sesame oil and vinegar, if desired.

Garnish with the lemon slices, cilantro and salt and pepper to taste.

Note: Pad Thai rice noodles or Asian rice noodle sticks work well, too. You can find them in the Asian section at most grocers.

DILL PESTO CUCUMBER NOODLE BOWLS

Do you love those little dill cucumber sandwiches? I do too! I could eat platefuls of them. So here's an idea: Why not make them into a pesto cucumber noodle bowl? Lighter, low carb and vegan friendly.

PREP TIME: 10 MINUTES • COOKING TIME: 0 MINUTES • SERVES: 1 TO 2

CREAMY DILL PESTO SAUCE
2 cups (80 g) dill with stem

½ cup (60 g) raw cashews

2 cloves garlic

1 small shallot (peeled) or about ¼ cup (40 g) red onion

¼ tsp fine sea salt or kosher salt, plus more to taste

Pepper

Pinch of cumin

½ lemon, juiced

1 tbsp (15 ml) Dijon mustard

¼ cup (60 ml) olive oil

BOWLS
1 cucumber

¼ cup (60 g) cooked peas or fava beans

1 tbsp (6 g) capers

Lemon wedge

Parmesan or nutritional yeast if vegan, optional, for topping

To make the pesto sauce, blend the dill, cashews, garlic, shallot, salt, pepper, cumin, lemon and Dijon mustard in a food processor or blender. Add the oil last, in a slow and steady stream, until a pesto is formed. You might need to stop a few times and scrape the sides.

Set aside ½ cup (120 ml) of the pesto and place the remaining pesto in a sealed container. This recipe makes 1 cup (240 ml), but you will only need ½ for the bowls.

Spiralize the cucumber and remove the excess water with paper towels.

In a medium bowl, combine the spiralized cucumber, pesto, peas and capers, and mix well. Place the cucumber mixture in 2 small bowls or keep as is in one large bowl, depending on how you would like to serve.

Give each bowl a squeeze of fresh lemon on top, and season with sea salt and pepper. Top with optional Parmesan or nutritional yeast.

Note: The extra pesto left over can be stored in an airtight container in the fridge for up to 5 days. But because it's so delicious on everything, it most likely will be eaten up before then!

GREEK CAULIFLOWER RICE PILAF BOWLS

Greek food is my favorite, and this Greek bowl is gonna rock your world! Think of this bowl as a deconstructed dolma, but lighter and lower in carbohydrates. We're using grape leaves as part of the pilaf, which brings a nice additional crunch to the cauliflower rice. Grape leaves are low calorie and packed with vitamin A. You can buy them canned or jarred at the grocery store, just be sure to rinse before using.

PREP TIME: 8 MINUTES • COOKING TIME: 10 MINUTES • SERVES: 2 TO 3

1 small to medium head cauliflower

3 to 4 tbsp (45 to 60 ml) olive oil

½ tsp garlic powder

¼ to ½ tsp fine sea salt or kosher salt, plus more to taste

½ tsp black pepper, plus more to taste

¼ cup (32 g) raw pumpkin seeds

1 cup (40 g) grape leaves

1 cup (160 g) cherry tomatoes

¼ cup (10 g) cilantro or basil

Small handful marinated green olives

½ lemon, juiced

Red pepper flakes, for garnish

Feta cheese crumbles, optional

Chopped dried fig or other dried fruit, optional

Preheat the oven to 400°F (204°C).

Remove the stem from the cauliflower and cut the cauliflower head into four or five sections. Place one or two sections of the cauliflower, depending on size, into a food processor and pulse until a cauliflower rice is formed, usually 3 or 4 pulses. Repeat for each section of the cauliflower.

Place the cauliflower rice in a large bowl. Add the olive oil, garlic powder, salt, pepper and pumpkin seeds, and toss to combine.

Place the cauliflower rice mix on an oiled baking sheet and spread out evenly. Bake for 10 minutes, tossing once during baking. Remove and let cool.

While the cauliflower is baking, prepare the grape leaves. Rinse the grape leaves with water to remove the excess salt. Press the grape leaves with a paper towel to remove the excess water. Set aside.

Chop or dice the cherry tomatoes, cilantro and green olives. Place in a bowl with the cauliflower rice, then add the grape leaves. Toss together, mixing well. Add a squeeze of lemon juice, salt and pepper to taste, and red pepper flakes. For a more authentic Mediterranean flavor, sprinkle with feta cheese crumbles and dried fig.

Divide into 2 to 3 bowls.

Note: Omit the feta topping for a vegan and Paleo friendly option.

QUICK ZESTY APPLE KIMCHI SALAD BOWLS

I have a mad crush on these kimchi bowls. The zingy Asian flavors are so invigorating and lively! No need to be intimidated with making real kimchi—this quick version is still healthy and nutritious, as it's packed with vitamin C and anti-inflammatory herbs and spices.

PREP TIME: 15 MINUTES • COOKING TIME: 0 MINUTES • SERVES: 1 TO 2

SAUCE
1 red Thai bird's eye pepper, sliced (see notes)

½ tsp lemongrass, finely chopped

¼ tsp ground ginger

1 tsp minced garlic

1 tbsp (15 ml) Sriracha or gluten-free chili sauce

1 to 2 tsp (5 to 10 ml) sesame oil

Pinch of pepper

Fine sea salt or kosher salt

1 tsp fish sauce (see notes)

1 tsp honey or coconut sugar

BOWLS
1 spiralized or shaved green apple

½ cup (60 g) sliced radish

1 small handful baby bok choy leaves or cabbages

1 sliced or shaved cucumber

TOPPINGS
1 green onion, green portion only, chopped

Handful of microgreens or sprouts

1 tbsp (10 g) sesame seeds

Lime juice

Protein of choice, optional (see notes)

To make the sauce, whisk the pepper, lemongrass, ginger, garlic, Sriracha, sesame oil, pepper, salt, fish sauce and honey in a large bowl.

For the bowls, mix the apple, radishes, bok choy and cucumber with the sauce. Let sit for 10 minutes or more at room temperature. Drain the brine if needed.

Divide the dressed salad evenly among 2 bowls, or use 1 large bowl. Top with the green onion, microgreens, sesame seeds, a splash of lime juice and protein, if desired.

Notes: You can sub a red jalapeño or cayenne pepper for the red Thai bird's eye pepper.

For fish sauce, look for a gluten-free variety in your grocery store. For a vegan option, use tamari.

For a Paleo option and protein, add shrimp, canned tuna, salmon or pork.

SHRIMP LAKSA CURRY BOWLS

Curry in a hurry anyone? That is one of my favorite sayings. These bowls take no time to make, plus they are full of spices that are rich with anti-inflammatory properties and lean protein.

PREP TIME: 30 MINUTES • COOKING TIME: 20 MINUTES • SERVES: 2 TO 3

4 to 5 oz (125 to 150 g) Asian rice noodles (see notes)

2 tbsp (30 ml) avocado oil or olive oil

3 tbsp (45 g) red curry paste

½ cup (120 ml) coconut milk, liquid

¼ tsp ground ginger

1 tsp minced garlic

1 tbsp (15 ml) tamari with splash of lime

1 tbsp (10 g) coconut or brown sugar

1 cup (220 g) raw medium shrimp (see notes)

½ lime, juiced

TOPPINGS

½ cup (20 g) or 1 small bunch chopped or torn cilantro, for garnish

1 to 2 Thai red chili peppers (see notes)

2 chopped green onions, stems removed, green part only

Fine sea salt or kosher salt, to taste

Pepper, to taste

Asian chili sauce, optional

Sesame seeds, optional

Place the rice noodles in a bowl of room temperature water and soak for 30 minutes. Drain and place back in the bowl. The less you soak, the more al dente they will be when cooked. It's up to you how long to soak, but I recommend at least 15 minutes.

In a large skillet or wok, heat the oil for 1 minute, then add the curry paste. Mix and cook for an additional minute. Add the coconut milk, ginger, garlic, tamari and coconut sugar to the skillet. Bring to a soft boil and stir until the sugar is dissolved, about 4 to 5 minutes.

Add the shrimp, squeeze in half a lime and stir-fry until the shrimp is no longer translucent. Add in the rice noodles, additional oil (if needed) and toss together in the skillet. Continue to cook over medium heat, coating the shrimp and noodles in the curry sauce until the shrimp are cooked through.

Divide into serving bowls, and top with the cilantro, peppers and green onion. Season with salt and pepper to taste. Top with the chili sauce and sesame seeds, if desired.

Notes: Pad Thai rice noodles or vermicelli rice noodles work best, and can be found in the Asian aisle.

For a vegan version, replace the shrimp with tofu, chickpeas or tempeh.

You can substitute the red chili peppers with another spicy red pepper of choice. Also keep in mind to deseed, if you'd like a less spicy dish.

LENTIL BROCCOLI TABBOULEH BOWLS

There are a lot of variations of tabbouleh out there, why not add one more? My version skips the grain and pumps up the veggies! The flavors are still light, crisp and refreshing, but with more plant protein and fiber. You can't beat that!

PREP TIME: 10 MINUTES • COOKING TIME: 20 MINUTES • SERVES: 2

1 cup (200 g) uncooked green or red lentils

Chicken or vegetable broth (gluten-free)

2 cups (350 g) broccoli florets or broccoli rabe, divided

½ to ⅔ cup (20 to 30 g) chopped parsley

4 mint leaves, plus extra for garnish

1 cup (160 g) grape tomatoes

¼ tsp fine sea salt or kosher salt, to taste, divided

¼ cup (40 g) chopped white onion or 3 greens, white portion, stem removed

½ lemon, plus extra slices for garnish

3 tbsp (45 ml) olive oil

Pepper, to taste

Feta crumbles, optional, for topping (see note)

2 to 3 tbsp (30 to 45 ml) kefir yogurt cheese topping, optional

Cook the lentils according to the package directions, replacing the water with broth. Once cooked, fluff with a fork, place in a bowl and set aside.

In a food processor, add 1 cup (230 g) of broccoli florets and pulse until a rice is formed. Remove, place in a bowl and repeat for the second cup of broccoli florets. Set aside.

Remove the stems of the parsley and mint, and place in the food processor. Add the tomatoes and pulse to chop together. Add ⅛ teaspoon of salt when you process the herbs and the tomatoes.

In the bowl with the broccoli rice, add the tomatoes and herbs, and mix in the white onion. Press out extra water from the herb and vegetable mixture after it's chopped and mixed.

Add the broccoli rice mixture to the lentil bowl, and add a squeeze of lemon juice, olive oil, remaining salt and pepper. Mix well, taste and adjust seasoning and olive oil as needed.

Serve in 2 bowls and garnish with sliced lemon and mint leaves. Top the bowl with feta crumbles and kefir yogurt cheese, if desired.

Note: Omit the feta and yogurt cheese for the vegan version.

SPICY PICKLED VEGGIE QUINOA BOWLS

My great-grandma used to make a delicious pickled carrot salad. I was always shocked at how she fit so many flavors into a vegetable salad. Now I know: The secret is in the sauce. Sweet, sour, tangy and whole-food based. Quinoa takes this from a simple salad to a full meal. Quinoa contains plant-based iron and all the essential amino acids—a smart way to bulk up a salad!

PREP TIME: 2 TO 24 HOURS • COOKING TIME: 0 MINUTES • SERVES: 3

SPICY SUGAR SAUCE
⅓ cup (80 ml) olive oil

¼ cup (60 ml) red wine vinegar

¼ cup (50 g) raw or coconut sugar

1 tsp ground mustard

½ tsp fine sea salt or kosher salt

½ tsp pepper

2 tsp (10 ml) Tabasco

1 tbsp (15 ml) agave or maple syrup

BOWL
4 cups (1.3 kg) cabbage slaw

2 large carrots, shaved into ribbons

1 jalapeño, sliced, seeds removed depending on level of spice desired

2 tsp (1 g) red pepper flakes

1¼ cups (200 g) cooked quinoa

2 to 3 tbsp (6 to 9 g) chopped green onion, green portion only

2 to 3 tbsp (12 to 17 g) capers

TOPPINGS
Handful of chopped cilantro

¼ cup (20 g) pepitas

1 lemon, sliced

Crushed red pepper flakes

Dollop of sour cream or yogurt cheese, optional (see note)

To make the spicy sugar sauce, whisk the olive oil, vinegar, sugar, mustard, salt, pepper, Tabasco and agave in a medium bowl to combine.

For the bowl, combine the cabbage slaw, carrots, jalapeño and red pepper flakes in a large bowl. Pour the spicy sugar sauce over the salad and mix to combine. Place in the fridge and marinate for 2 to 24 hours.

Once marinated, place the salad in a large bowl with the quinoa, green onion and capers. Top with the cilantro, pepitas, lemon, red pepper flakes and a dollop of sour cream, if desired.

Note: For a vegan option, omit the sour cream.

CREAMY AVOCADO TUNA ZOODLE BOWLS

This is not your mama's tuna salad, y'all: it's way better! Okay, I may be biased. But it is WAY better for you. The creamy avocado sauce and zucchini noodles make this classic dish lower carb, high protein and there's minimal cooking required.

PREP TIME: 10 MINUTES • COOKING TIME: 2 TO 3 MINUTES • SERVES: 2 TO 3

AVOCADO SAUCE
½ large avocado, skin and pit removed

½ tbsp (8 ml) Dijon mustard

½ cup (110 ml) real mayo or plain yogurt (see notes)

1 tbsp (15 ml) lemon juice

3 to 4 tbsp (45 to 60 ml) olive oil

½ tsp minced garlic, about 1 clove

½ tsp pepper

¼ tsp fine sea salt or kosher salt, or to taste

1 tsp crushed red pepper flakes

BOWLS
2 medium zucchinis, spiralized or julienned

⅔ to 1 cup (25 to 40 g) greens, kale or spinach

2 tbsp (30 ml) water

5 oz (140 g) canned tuna, drained

1 cup (150 g) peas, cooked

1 green onion, chopped with white end removed

Chopped uncured bacon, optional, for topping

¼ cup (45 g) shredded Parmesan, optional, for topping (see notes)

To make the avocado sauce, combine the avocado, Dijon mustard, mayo, lemon juice, olive oil, garlic, pepper, salt and red pepper flakes in a food processor or blender, and blend until creamy. Adjust the salt and pepper to taste, if needed.

For the bowls, gently press or squeeze as much water out of the spiralized zucchini as possible with a paper towel. Drain the water and pat the zucchini noodles dry to remove the excess water. Place in a large bowl and toss with half of the avocado sauce, coating evenly.

In a saucepan on the stove, add the greens with the water and cook, covered, over medium heat until the greens are softened, 2 to 3 minutes. For the microwave, cook the greens for 20 to 30 seconds in a microwave-safe dish.

In a medium bowl, combine the other half of the avocado sauce with the tuna, mixing well.

Divide the creamy zoodles evenly among 2 to 3 serving bowls and scoop ¼ cup (50 g) or more of tuna salad on top of each.

Add ⅓ cup (60 g) of steamed greens to each bowl, or place on the side. Top each bowl with the peas and green onion.

Garnish with the chopped bacon and Parmesan, if desired. Season with extra red pepper flakes, salt and pepper.

Notes: I recommend using real mayonnaise with olive oil or avocado oil for the best flavor. It also keeps this meal perfectly Paleo.

Omit the Parmesan topping for a Paleo friendly option.

PLANT-POWERED BOWLS

Many people think that plant-based recipes and vegetarian recipes are boring, bland and lacking protein. What a HUGE misconception. In fact, I've made several plant-based meals for my meat-eating husband and three brothers. And guess what? They never knew!

Here's a little trick you need to know about making plant-based meals flavorful and balanced. Focus on using a variety of plants in each dish. This includes properly prepared legumes, nuts, seeds, vegetables, fruits, leafy greens and cultured soy. They all have their place in a whole-foods-based diet. They all contain immunity-boosting nutrients and they all work in synergy to create hearty and wholesome meals! I think you will agree once you try my Moroccan Roasted Veggie Power Bowls (page 90) or the Loaded Sweet Potato Nacho Salad Bowls (page 101).

KALE PESTO SWEET POTATO SPAGHETTI BOWLS

Kale, almonds and sweet potato make the perfect synergy food combo. All of the ingredients are rich in antioxidants to boost immunity. Perfect for fall or winter, or when you're feeling under the weather!

PREP TIME: 10 MINUTES • COOKING TIME: 10 MINUTES • SERVES: 2

PESTO

2 cups (80 g) kale, chopped, stems removed

½ cup (85 g) almonds, toasted or roasted

⅓ cup (50 g) nutritional yeast, plus more for topping

2 tsp (6 g) minced garlic

1 cup (40 g) fresh basil

½ lemon, juiced

½ tsp fine sea salt or kosher salt

Pinch of black pepper

⅓ cup (80 ml) olive oil

BOWL

1 medium sweet potato, spiralized

1 tbsp (15 ml) water

1 tbsp (15 ml) olive oil

2 oz (60 g) olives, chopped

3 oz (90 g) canned or roasted chickpeas (see notes)

Lemon wedge

Fresh basil leaves, for garnish

Sprinkle of crushed red pepper flakes

To make the pesto, combine the kale, almonds, nutritional yeast, garlic, basil, lemon juice, salt and pepper in a food processor. Pulse until somewhat blended, then scrape down the sides. Place the food processor on medium speed and slowly add the olive oil. Blend until a pesto texture is formed. Add additional salt and pepper to taste. Remove from the food processor and place in a bowl.

In a microwave-safe bowl, add the sweet potato noodles with the water and cover with a paper towel. Steam in the microwave for 1 minute until softened, then drain off the excess water.

In a medium saucepan, add the olive oil, the sweet potato noodles, ½ cup (125 g) of the kale almond pesto and the olives.

Cook over medium heat for 5 minutes, stirring often, until the sweet potato noodles are cooked. Add to the serving bowls.

For the vegan option, top each bowl with the chickpeas and additional nutritional yeast. Garnish with lemon, basil leaves and crushed red pepper flakes. Season with salt and pepper to taste.

Note: For a Paleo option, swap out the chickpeas for 3 to 4 ounces (85 to 115 g) of cooked sliced chicken or cooked ground beef.

MEDITERRANEAN LAYERED LENTIL SALAD BOWLS

Layers and layers of flavor and health! That's what I should have called this bowl. Lentils, olives, leafy greens and that's just the start. You'll feel content and nourished after you dive into this bowl.

PREP TIME: 10 MINUTES • COOKING TIME: 0 MINUTES • SERVES: 4

BOWLS

3 to 5 cups (120 to 200 g) leafy greens (spinach, kale or red lettuce)

2 cups (200 g) chopped green cabbage

2 cups (400 g) cooked green lentils (see notes)

1 to 2 cups (160 to 320 g) grape tomatoes, sliced

1 oz (30 g) sun-dried raisins

1 oz (30 g) marinated olives

⅓ cup (40 g) kefir yogurt cheese (see notes)

TOPPINGS

Crushed red pepper flakes

Handful fresh watercress or other bitter greens

Lemon slices

Olive oil

Vinegar

Crumbled or Parmesan cheese (see note)

⅛ to ¼ tsp fine sea salt or kosher salt, to taste

⅛ to ¼ tsp pepper, to taste

In a large serving bowl or 4 separate bowls, arrange the leafy greens and top with the green cabbage. Add the lentils, followed by the tomatoes, raisins, olives and yogurt cheese.

Top with the crushed red pepper flakes, watercress and lemon slices. Drizzle with the olive oil and vinegar, and sprinkle with the Parmesan cheese. Season with salt and pepper to taste.

Notes: The green lentils are best cooked in broth for more flavor.

If you can't find kefir yogurt cheese, you can use organic sour cream mixed with 1 tablespoon (15 ml) of olive oil and lemon juice.

For a vegan option, omit the Parmesan cheese and the kefir yogurt cheese and substitute nutritional yeast.

CARROT SPAGHETTI ALLA PUTTANESCA BOWLS

Spiralized carrots in zesty Italian tomato sauce. This easy, one-pot recipe uses simple real food ingredients already in your pantry. Don't you love that? It's the perfect meatless meal that will nourish kids and adults alike!

PREP TIME: 10 MINUTES • COOKING TIME: 10 MINUTES • SERVES: 1 TO 2

3 large carrots

1 sweet potato or purple yam

3 to 4 tbsp (33 to 45 g) olives, pitted and diced

½ tsp minced garlic

1 tsp capers or artichokes (can substitute anchovy paste for Paleo)

½ to 1 tbsp (8 to 15 ml) olive oil

½ to ⅔ cup (75 to 100 g) chopped onion

1 cup (160 g) cherry tomatoes

2 tbsp (30 ml) white wine

1 to 2 tbsp (15 to 30 ml) vegetable broth, optional

¼ tsp Italian seasoning

Fine sea salt or kosher salt, to taste

Pepper, to taste

Crushed red pepper flakes, optional, for topping

1 to 2 tbsp (2.5 to 5 g) fresh basil

Grated Parmesan cheese, optional, for topping (see note)

2 to 3 tbsp (12 to 17 g) capers, optional, for topping

Spiralize or julienne cut the carrots and sweet potato. Add to a microwave-safe bowl and microwave for 1 minute. Set aside.

In a small bowl, mash the olives, garlic and capers. Alternatively, you can finely chop the olives, garlic and capers and mix together. Set aside.

In a sauté pan, add the oil and the onion, and cook over high heat until fragrant, 2 minutes.

Add the tomatoes and cook 2 minutes until mixed and softened.

Stir in the olives, garlic and caper mixture. Add the white wine, broth and Italian seasoning, cooking over medium heat for a few minutes.

Add the cooked tomato mixture to the spiralized veggies, tossing well. Season with salt, pepper and crushed red pepper flakes. Serve in 1 large bowl or 2 small bowls. Top with the basil, Parmesan and capers.

Note: For a vegan or Paleo option, omit the Parmesan cheese.

MOROCCAN ROASTED VEGGIE POWER BOWLS

Harissa recipes vary between countries and regions, but most include a blend of hot chile peppers (regular or smoked), garlic, cumin, coriander, caraway and mint or ginger. All are powerful spices that boost nutrition.

PREP TIME: 10 MINUTES • COOKING TIME: 25 MINUTES • SERVES: 3 TO 4

ROASTED VEGGIES

8 oz (230 g) broccoli florets (fresh or frozen)

8 oz (230 g) cauliflower florets (fresh or frozen)

1½ cups (300 g) cooked or canned chickpeas, drained

⅓ cup (80 ml) olive oil

1 to 1½ tbsp (2 to 4 g) harissa dry spice seasoning (see notes)

1 tsp minced garlic

½ to 1 tsp fine sea salt or kosher salt

½ to 1 tsp pepper

BOWLS

2 cups (80 g) chopped leafy greens

2 cups (150 g) cooked black or green lentils, for plating

1 chopped green onion, or ¼ cup (40 g) chopped red onion

⅔ cup (80 g) sliced radish

TOPPINGS

Sliced lemon

⅔ cup (100 g) crumbled goat cheese or feta cheese (see notes)

Fresh cilantro

Crushed red pepper flakes

Garlic salt or garlic powder, to taste

Olive oil

Balsamic vinegar

1 tbsp (15 ml) fresh lemon juice

Preheat the oven to 425°F (218°C). Line or oil a baking sheet.

To make the roasted veggies, toss the broccoli, cauliflower and chickpeas with the olive oil, harissa, garlic, salt and pepper. Layer on a baking sheet and roast for 20 to 25 minutes.

For the bowls, layer equal amounts of the leafy greens, followed by the lentils, green onion, radishes and roasted veggies in each. Top each bowl with the sliced lemon, goat cheese, cilantro, red pepper flakes and garlic salt. Drizzle each bowl with the olive oil, balsamic vinegar and a squeeze of lemon.

Notes: If you don't have harissa seasoning, you can make your own. Mix together 1 tablespoon (8 g) of hot paprika combined with ¼ teaspoon each of caraway seeds, cumin, garlic powder, pepper, sea salt, cinnamon and ginger.

For a vegan option, omit the cheese.

For added protein, toss chopped hard-boiled egg, chicken or salmon on each bowl to boost protein content and make it a main meal!

AVOCADO PESTO MEXICAN PASTA BOWLS

This bowl is basically every superfood made into a Mexican dish. Black beans, avocado, cumin, beets or sweet potato noodles, tomatoes and the list goes on . . . that's probably why I love it! It's grain-free, quick to make and vegan friendly! Plus, the avocado pesto makes a great dip or gluten-free toast topper.

PREP TIME: 10 MINUTES • COOKING TIME: 15 MINUTES • SERVES: 2

AVOCADO PESTO
½ avocado

⅓ cup (50 g) red onion, chopped

⅓ cup (15 g) fresh cilantro

½ tsp minced garlic

½ tsp cumin

3 tbsp (25 g) pine nuts or raw cashews

¼ cup (60 ml) olive oil

1 tbsp (15 ml) fresh lemon juice

Fine sea salt or kosher salt, to taste, plus more for bowls

Pepper, to taste

SWEET POTATOES
2 small purple sweet potatoes, regular sweet potatoes or three purple beets, spiralized or julienned

1 to 2 tsp (5 to 10 ml) oil

BOWLS
⅔ cup (100 g) cooked corn

¼ tsp cumin

Sliced jalapeño

2 to 3 tbsp (25 to 40 g) black bean salsa or pico de gallo (see note)

Fresh cilantro, for garnish

1 lemon wedge, for garnish

To make the avocado pesto, combine the avocado, onion, cilantro, garlic, cumin, pine nuts, olive oil, lemon juice, salt and pepper in a food processor. Blend until a creamy pesto is formed. Scrape the sides of the food processor if needed and keep blending until creamy. If it's too thick, add 1 to 2 tablespoons (15 to 30 ml) more oil to thin out the pesto.

Preheat the oven to 425°F (218°C). Line or oil a baking sheet.

For the sweet potatoes, toss the sweet potato noodles with the oil. Layer on a baking sheet and roast for 10 to 15 minutes, or until crispy and slightly tender. For the sweet potatoes, you will want to bake the noodles closer to 15 minutes or until al dente. If you are using spiralized beets, they should bake closer to 10 minutes. Set aside to cool.

For the bowls, combine ½ cup (120 g) of the avocado pesto with the cooked spiralized sweet potato noodles, corn, salt and cumin in a large bowl. Toss all of the ingredients together, coating well. Reserve the rest of the avocado pesto for topping.

Divide the coated sweet potatoes noodles equally between 2 bowls. Top with jalapeño, black bean salsa, cilantro, extra avocado pesto and a lemon wedge.

Note: If you don't have salsa to top, feel free to add fresh chopped tomatoes and onions instead.

SUMMER DETOX QUINOA SALAD BOWLS

You know those days where you just feel fried? Whether it's from fun in the sun or mental stress, these bowls are the perfect cure. They have healing power from cherries, mint, lemon, spinach and asparagus, plus, just the right boost of protein from both quinoa and almonds.

PREP TIME: 10 MINUTES • COOKING TIME: LESS THAN 1 MINUTE • SERVES: 1 TO 2

5 large asparagus spears

½ lemon, juiced

2 to 3 mint leaves

1 bunch large spinach leaves

1 tbsp (15 ml) water

1 cup (160 g) cooked quinoa (see note)

1 tbsp (5 g) crushed almonds

2 cups (200 g) cherries, chopped

½ cup (65 g) cucumber slices

1 large shaved carrot

Broccoli sprouts, for garnish

Lemon wedges, for garnish

Lime wedges, for garnish

1 tbsp (15 ml) avocado oil or cold pressed extra virgin olive oil

Balsamic vinegar

Fine sea salt or kosher salt, to taste

Pepper, to taste

In a food processor, blend the asparagus, lemon and mint leaves until chopped and mixed. Remove from the blender and set aside.

In a microwave-safe bowl, add the spinach with the water. Steam in microwave for about 30 seconds.

In a large bowl or 2 small bowls, arrange the spinach leaves, followed by the quinoa, almonds, cherries, cucumber, carrots and broccoli sprouts. Top with the asparagus mixture, then garnish with the lemon and lime wedges. Drizzle with the avocado oil and balsamic vinegar, and season with salt and pepper to taste.

Note: For best flavor, cook quinoa in broth instead of water.

TEMPEH TACO SWEET POTATO SPAGHETTI BOWLS

Tempeh is so versatile and nourishing. It's another fermented soy superfood that is easier to digest, is rich in iron, fiber and protein, and is one of my favorite real food meat substitutes!

PREP TIME: 10 MINUTES • COOKING TIME: 7 TO 8 MINUTES • SERVES: 2

TEMPEH
8 oz (230 g) gluten-free tempeh, crumbled

4 oz (115 g) green chiles or salsa verde

1 jalapeño or red chile pepper

¼ cup (40 g) chopped onion

½ tsp garlic

Olive oil

½ tsp cumin

Fine sea salt or kosher salt, to taste

Pepper, to taste

SWEET POTATO
1 sweet potato, spiralized

1 tbsp (15 ml) broth or water

BOWLS
1 tsp oil

⅓ cup (50 g) chopped onion

⅔ cup (135 g) cooked black beans

⅔ cup (100 g) cooked corn

TOPPINGS
Cilantro, chopped

Handful cooked chickpeas

Avocado, sliced, or guacamole

Crushed red pepper flakes

Olive oil, optional

Lime wedges, optional

Nutritional yeast or sour cream, optional (see note)

To make the tempeh, combine the tempeh, green chiles, jalapeño, onion, garlic, olive oil, cumin, salt and pepper in a food processor or blender. Blend until the mixture is thoroughly combined and the tempeh has a minced texture.

For the sweet potato, microwave the potato in a microwave-safe bowl with the broth for 1 minute. Remove from the microwave and combine with the tempeh and veggie mixture.

For the bowls, heat the oil in a sauté pan and add the onion, cooking for 2 minutes until translucent, over medium heat. Add the black beans, corn and tempeh–sweet potato mixture. Cook for 3 to 4 minutes or until the sweet potato noodles are cooked. Divide equally between 2 bowls.

Top the bowls with the cilantro, chickpeas, avocado and crushed red pepper flakes. Drizzle with olive oil and a squeeze of lime, if desired. Season with salt and pepper to taste.

Note: If not vegan, feel free to add sour cream on top. Vegans can get a "cheesy" taste by adding nutritional yeast.

KOREAN BBQ CHICKPEA BENTO BOWLS

If you love Korean BBQ, I think you'll love this plant-based bento bowl version. Perfect for lunches and kid friendly dinners, this veggie dish is rich in protein, fiber and plant-based iron.

PREP TIME: 10 MINUTES • COOKING TIME: 20 MINUTES • SERVES: 2 TO 3

MARINADE

3 tbsp (45 ml) tamari

2 tbsp (30 ml) water

2 tbsp (30 ml) tomato sauce

2 tsp (10 ml) honey or coconut sugar (see notes)

¼ tsp ground ginger

¼ tsp pepper

1 tsp minced garlic

1 tbsp (15 ml) sesame oil

2 to 3 tbsp (30 to 45 ml) chopped green onion or red onion

1 (15-oz [400-g]) can cooked chickpeas

½ cup (80 g) unshelled cooked edamame, optional

BOWLS

2 cups (420 g) cooked rice

1 cup (340 g) chopped Brussels sprouts or shredded cabbage (see notes)

1 zucchini, ribbon cut

1 carrot, ribbon cut

1 cup (160 g) sliced grape tomatoes

TOPPINGS

½ lime, juiced

1 to 2 tbsp (10 to 20 g) sesame seeds

½ tbsp (1 g) crushed red pepper flakes

Fine sea salt

Pepper

1 cup (40 g) microgreens or sprouts

Handful of fresh cilantro

Preheat the oven to 400°F (204°C). Line a baking sheet with foil.

To make the Korean BBQ marinade, combine the tamari, water, tomato sauce, honey, ginger, pepper, garlic, sesame oil and green onion in a medium-size bowl. Add the chickpeas and edamame, if desired, to the marinade bowl and toss thoroughly to cover. Reserve 1 to 2 tablespoons (15 to 30 ml) of the marinade for topping the bowl.

Spread out the chickpea mixture on the prepared baking sheet. Roast for 15 to 20 minutes, turning once, until the chickpeas are crispy. Remove from the oven and set aside. Let the chickpeas cool while preparing the bowls.

For the bowls, divide the cooked rice into 2 bowls, or 3 bowls for smaller portions. Top the rice bowls with the Brussels sprouts, zucchini, carrot and tomatoes, followed by the BBQ roasted chickpeas.

Squeeze the fresh lime juice on top of each bowl, then sprinkle with the sesame seeds and red pepper flakes. Season with salt or pepper, to taste, and garnish with the microgreens and fresh cilantro. For more BBQ zing, drizzle the reserved marinade sauce on top, or swap it out for your favorite BBQ sauce.

Notes: For a vegan option, omit the honey and use coconut sugar.

This bowl is full of flavor and great texture. Feel free to roast the chopped Brussels sprouts along with the chickpeas. This adds a smoky flavor to the vegetables.

LOADED SWEET POTATO NACHO SALAD BOWLS

I remember the first time I made baked sweet potato chips. I couldn't believe how simple they were to make—so much more flavor than fried, too! That's when I decided that sweet potato nachos were definitely going to happen. Can you believe it, a loaded nacho recipe that serves as a healthy balanced meal?

PREP TIME: 10 MINUTES • COOKING TIME: 20 MINUTES • SERVES: 2

SWEET POTATO CHIPS
1 large sweet potato, sliced into thin chips

1 tbsp (15 ml) olive oil

Pinch of fine sea salt or kosher salt

Pinch of pepper

½ tsp garlic powder

1 oz (30 g) sliced aged cheddar

BOWLS
3 cups (120 g) greens

1 cup (200 g) white cannellini or black beans, cooked and drained

½ large avocado, sliced

TOPPINGS
1 jalapeño, sliced

1 green onion, green portion only, sliced

⅓ cup (15 g) chopped or torn cilantro

Avocado La Crema Sauce (see Baja Fish Taco Bowl, page 118), optional

Tabasco, optional

Grated Parmesan cheese, optional

Crushed red pepper flakes, optional

Preheat the oven to 400°F (204°C). Line a baking sheet with foil or coat it well with cooking oil.

To make the sweet potato chips, toss the sweet potato slices with olive oil, salt, pepper and garlic powder.

Place the sweet potato chips on the baking sheet, and arrange the cheese slices on top. Bake for 20 minutes, or until the cheese is melted and the edges of the sweet potatoes are crispy. Broil for the last few minutes for extra-crispy chips. Remove and let cool slightly.

For the bowls, divide the sweet potato chips evenly between the 2 serving bowls. Top with the greens, beans and avocado. Top each bowl with the jalapeño, green onions and cilantro. Season with salt and pepper, to taste. Drizzle on the avocado sauce, if desired, and Tabasco. Sprinkle with the Parmesan and crushed red pepper flakes, if desired.

CURRIED SATAY VEGGIE BOWLS

Revitalize plain veggies with this delightfully creamy satay bowl. Loaded with healthy fats and antioxidant-rich spices, you'll get loads of health benefits in every bite. Rainbow-colored veggies and Thai-inspired flavors make this dish one of my favorites!

PREP TIME: 10 MINUTES • COOKING TIME: 2 TO 3 MINUTES • SERVES: 1 TO 2

SATAY SAUCE
1 (15-oz [425-g]) can chickpeas

1 tbsp (15 g) red curry paste

1 tsp minced garlic

Pinch fresh grated ginger, or ¼ tsp ground

1 tbsp (15 ml) avocado or coconut oil

1 tsp mustard

2 to 3 tbsp (45 ml) coconut milk

1 tbsp (12 g) creamy natural peanut butter

Dash of lime juice or rice vinegar

Fine sea salt or kosher salt, to taste

Pepper, to taste

BOWLS
2 small zucchinis (see note)

1 tsp olive oil

1 tsp tamari

TOPPINGS
Handful ribbon-cut or julienne-sliced veggies (carrot and summer squash work great)

Cilantro

Crushed nuts

Crushed red pepper flakes

Sriracha, optional

To make the satay sauce, combine the chickpeas, red curry paste, garlic, ginger, oil, mustard and 2 tablespoons (30 ml) of coconut milk in a food processor or blender. Blend until mixed. With the food processor on low, slowly add the peanut butter, vinegar, salt and pepper. Blend again until creamy. For thinner sauce, add 1 tablespoon (15 ml) or more of coconut milk. Stop and scrape sides once or twice if needed. Put the sauce in a bowl and set aside. Extra sauce can be stored in the fridge for up to 5 days.

For the bowls, spiralize the zucchini, then press with a paper towel to remove the excess water.

In a large skillet or wok, add the oil and stir-fry the zucchini noodles with the tamari for 2 to 3 minutes, or until zucchini noodles are soft, but not mushy. Remove and place zucchini noodles in one large serving bowl or 2 smaller serving bowls.

Drizzle each bowl with the creamy satay sauce and top with a handful of ribbon-cut vegetables, cilantro, crushed nuts and crushed red pepper flakes. Add a dash of Sriracha, if desired.

Once you add the sauce, serve immediately. Due to the high water content in the zucchini noodles, the sauce will become soupy if left to sit. Simply add more zucchini noodles to thicken the sauce, or spoon out a few tablespoons of liquid. But not to worry: even the thinned out sauce is delicious with the noodles. Totally slurp worthy!

Note: To make zucchini noodles without a spiralizer, simply julienne slice them or use a potato peeler to create long flat shavings or ribbons.

CHILI GARLIC CAULIFLOWER RISOTTO BOWLS

A risotto bowl is an easy plant-based dish to satisfy that comfort-food craving! A healthy, quick recipe with a spicy, creamy, nondairy sauce and cauliflower rice acting as the risotto, all cooked in one pan! Now that's what I call guiltless gourmet.

PREP TIME: 10 MINUTES • COOKING TIME: 10 MINUTES • SERVES: 3

CHILI GARLIC CREAM SAUCE
1 to 2 tbsp (15 to 30 ml) chili sauce or paste, or Sriracha

1 avocado

Pinch of pepper

2 to 3 tsp (7 to 10 g) minced garlic

½ cup (120 ml) coconut milk or almond milk

½ tbsp (10 g) fresh grated ginger or ½ tsp ground

1 tsp red chili pepper flakes

¼ tsp fine sea salt or kosher salt, plus more to taste

2 tsp (10 ml) gluten-free tamari or gluten-free Worcestershire sauce (see notes)

1 to 2 tbsp (15 to 30 ml) honey or agave

2 tbsp (30 ml) water or oil

CAULIFLOWER RISOTTO
14 oz (400 g) or 1 small head cauliflower, stems and leaves removed

1 to 2 tsp (5 to 10 ml) olive or coconut oil

1 tsp minced garlic

¼ cup (40 g) yellow onion, chopped

2 to 3 tbsp (25 to 40 g) diced red bell peppers

½ cup (120 ml) coconut milk

Pepper, to taste

Lemon or lime juice

1 small green or banana pepper, sliced

1 bunch basil or Thai basil, chopped

¼ cup (40 g) crushed toasted or roasted nuts

Cucumber slices, for topping

Cilantro or additional herbs, for garnish, optional

To make the chili garlic cream sauce, combine the chili sauce, avocado, pepper, garlic and coconut milk in a blender. Blend well, then add the ginger, red chili pepper flakes, salt, tamari, honey and water. Thin the sauce by adding in 2 to 4 tablespoons (30 to 60 ml) of water or coconut milk. Adjust the sauce for sweetness.

For the cauliflower risotto, place half of the cauliflower in a food processor and pulse until it is riced. Place in a medium-size bowl and repeat with the other half. Set aside.

In a small sauté pan, heat the oil over medium heat, then add the garlic and onion. Sauté until fragrant, about 1 to 2 minutes.

Add the riced cauliflower and red peppers. Cook over medium heat for 2 to 3 minutes, then add the coconut milk. If you want a creamier salad, add an additional 2 to 3 tablespoons (30 to 45 ml) of coconut cream. Continue to cook, coating the cauliflower rice risotto, about 5 minutes.

Add the salt, pepper and a dash of lemon juice. Remove from the heat. Place the risotto in a large bowl or 3 separate bowls and top with the sliced green pepper, chopped basil, crushed nuts and cucumber.

Drizzle the chili garlic cream sauce over each bowl before serving. Garnish with the cilantro.

Notes: This bowl is great as a side dish or complete meal topped with a protein of your choice: tofu, grilled shrimp, chicken, meatballs or even egg!

For Whole30-compliant tamari sauce, use coconut aminos.

THAI MANGO EDAMAME NOODLE SALAD BOWLS

This dish is sweet and spicy and packed full of wholesome carbohydrates and plant-based protein.

PREP TIME: 40 MINUTES • COOKING TIME: 2 MINUTES • SERVES: 3 TO 4

CHILI MANGO YOGURT SAUCE
⅓ cup (60 g) mango, peeled and diced

½ medium avocado, peeled and diced

2 cloves garlic

¼ cup (40 g) shallot, chopped

½ cup (80 g) cherry tomatoes, diced

⅓ cup (15 g) cilantro, chopped

⅓ cup (80 g) plain yogurt (see notes)

2 tbsp (30 ml) Asian sweet red chili sauce (see notes)

½ tsp ground cumin

1 tbsp (15 ml) sesame or olive oil

Fine sea salt or kosher salt, to taste

Pepper, to taste

Fresh lime juice

BOWLS
4 oz (115 g) Asian rice noodles

1 cup (150 g) edamame, shelled (if frozen, thaw)

TOPPINGS
Thinly sliced bell pepper

Chopped green onion (green portion only)

¼ cup (40 g) crushed smoked or roasted almonds or peanuts

1 to 2 tbsp (10 to 20 g) sesame seeds

Chopped cilantro, for garnish

1 tbsp (15 ml) gluten-free tamari

Lime juice

1 tbsp (15 ml) Thai sweet chili sauce

To make the sauce, combine the mango, avocado, garlic, shallot, tomatoes, cilantro and yogurt in a food processor, blending until mixed. Add the Asian sweet red chili sauce, cumin and oil, and blend again. Taste, and add the salt and pepper to taste. Blend, then stop and scrape the sides if needed. Add a dash of lime juice. Blend once more until a creamy thick consistency is formed.

For the bowls, soak the rice noodles in hot water for 30 minutes. Rinse with cold water and check for tenderness. If they are still not tender enough, place them in boiling water for 2 minutes. Rinse with cold water and place in a medium bowl with the edamame. Toss with ⅔ cup (162 g) or more of the sauce.

Divide evenly among the serving bowls. Top with the bell pepper, green onion, nuts, sesame seeds and cilantro. Drizzle with the tamari, a splash of lime juice, Thai sweet chili sauce and any extra reserved sauce, if desired. Season with salt.

Notes: For extra protein, feel free to add tofu, chicken, shrimp or egg.

To make the sauce vegan, use nondairy plain yogurt. For a Paleo option, use Greek yogurt.

In place of the Asian sweet red chili sauce, you can use garlic chili sauce or Thai sweet chili sauce. Make sure to check that the ingredients are gluten-free. Thai Kitchen has a great gluten-free chili sauce.

SWEET POTATO PICADILLO BOWLS

Picadillo is a Cuban style hash usually made with meat and layers of olives, capers and raisins. This vegan picadillo recipe uses a similar combo of sweet and savory but with plant-based ingredients.

PREP TIME: 10 MINUTES • COOKING TIME: 30 TO 40 MINUTES • SERVES: 4

ROASTED CHICKPEAS
1 (15-oz [425-g]) can chickpeas, drained and rinsed

¼ tsp cumin

Pinch of fine sea salt or kosher salt, plus more to taste

½ tsp minced garlic

¼ tsp cayenne

½ to 1 tbsp (8 to 15 ml) olive oil

BOWLS
1 tbsp (15 ml) olive oil

1 small onion or 1⅓ cups (200 g) chopped onion

1 bell pepper or sweet pepper, chopped

3 cloves garlic or 1 tsp minced

1 tsp cumin

1 tsp oregano

2 bay leaves

¼ tsp cinnamon

1 cup (250 g) stewed tomatoes (drained if using canned)

1 tbsp (15 ml) red wine vinegar

2 tbsp (30 g) tomato paste

1 sweet potato, peeled and cubed

Black pepper

2 to 3 tbsp (12 to 17 g) raisins or dried cranberries, optional

¼ tsp chili powder or cayenne, optional

½ cup (90 g) green olives, sliced, and ½ tbsp (8 ml) brine from olive jar

Cilantro, optional, for garnish

Preheat the oven to 400°F (204°C). Line or oil a baking sheet

To make the roasted chickpeas, toss the chickpeas with cumin, salt, garlic, cayenne and olive oil. Place on a baking tray and roast for 12 to 15 minutes. Remove from the oven and set aside.

For the bowls, heat the olive oil in a large pan or skillet over medium heat. Add the onion, pepper and garlic, and sauté until the onion starts to caramelize, around 2 minutes or so.

In the pan or skillet, add the cumin, oregano, bay leaves and cinnamon. Cook until fragrant, another 3 to 4 minutes. Add the stewed tomatoes, red wine vinegar, tomato paste, sweet potato, salt and pepper, mixing to combine. Cook the mixture, partially covered, for 10 minutes or until the potatoes are cooked and somewhat tender.

Add the raisins, chili powder, olives and roasted chickpeas. Stew on the stovetop for another 5 to 10 minutes. Add the olive brine the last few minutes of cooking.

Divide evenly in serving bowls and garnish with cilantro, if desired.

WINTER'S DELIGHT BUDDHA BOWLS

This wholesome Winter's Delight Buddha Bowl recipe is filled with superfood winter produce and is a delicious way to get a variety of nutrients and plant-based iron into your diet. It's also one of my favorite vegan bowl recipes that bring comfort and nourishment to the body on a cold day. The creamy apple cider dressing is a staple recipe I use on many winter dishes.

PREP TIME: 10 MINUTES • COOKING TIME: 25 MINUTES • SERVES: 2 TO 3

CREAMY APPLE CIDER DRESSING
¼ cup (60 g) tahini or almond butter

½ tbsp (8 ml) organic apple cider vinegar

¼ tsp sea salt

1 tbsp (15 ml) maple syrup

2 to 3 tbsp (30 to 45 ml) warm almond milk or coconut milk

¼ tsp cumin, optional

¼ tsp mustard powder, optional

Dash of black pepper

BOWLS
2 cups (400 g) chickpeas

1 cup (180 g) peeled chopped butternut squash

2 cups (240 g) small beets, peeled and spiralized or diced (see notes)

⅓ cup (50 g) chopped shallot or red onion

2 tbsp (30 ml) olive oil

¼ tsp cumin

¼ tsp sea salt

Pinch of garlic powder

1 cup (35 g) fresh cranberries

1 bunch winter kale, stems removed

2 radicchio heads, chopped

1 cup (185 g) cooked quinoa

1 to 2 tbsp (10 to 20 g) pepita seeds

1 orange, sliced and peeled

Preheat the oven to 400°F (204°C). Line a baking sheet or roasting pan with parchment paper.

To make the dressing, whisk together the tahini, vinegar, salt, maple syrup, almond milk, cumin, mustard powder and pepper in a small bowl until creamy. Set aside.

For the bowls, toss the chickpeas, squash, beets and shallot in the olive oil. Add the cumin, salt and garlic powder. Toss again.

On the baking sheet, spread the chickpea mixture, making sure it's even. Scatter the fresh cranberries around the vegetables. Place in the oven and roast for 20 to 25 minutes, checking the squash and beets at the 10-minute mark, and flipping them if the bottoms get too dark.

In a large bowl, add the kale and radicchio. Top with the cooked quinoa, followed by the roasted vegetables and cranberries.

Garnish with the pepita seeds and orange slices, and season with additional sea salt and pepper. Drizzle with the apple cider dressing.

Serve from one large bowl or divide into 2 or 3 small bowls.

Notes: If you have extra apple cider dressing, you can store it, covered, in the fridge for up to 7 days.

Spiralized beets are more delicate and will cook faster than chopped beets. In this case, be sure to check the cooking progress halfway. Another option is to place the spiralized beets on a separate pan, but to cook them at the same time as the other vegetables.

CREAMY RED PEPPER CARROT PAPPARDELLE PASTA BOWLS

I love pasta! I'm so glad that I can easily re-create a grain-free version with carrot ribbons. It has the same texture, more flavor and is naturally gluten-free. You have my full permission to hog the pasta bowl tonight, especially with that creamy red pepper sauce.

PREP TIME: 24 HOURS · COOKING TIME: 20 MINUTES · SERVES: 2

CREAMY RED PEPPER SAUCE
⅔ cup (75 g) cashews

1½ cups (355 ml) purified water

2 roasted red peppers

3 to 4 cloves garlic, peeled

1 tsp onion powder

½ to 1 tsp fine sea salt or kosher salt

½ to 1 tsp black pepper

1 to 2 green onions, white stems only, or 3 tbsp (30 g) white onion, chopped

½ tbsp (8 ml) olive oil

½ lemon, juiced

1 tbsp (15 ml) Dijon or honey mustard

Coconut cream or almond milk, optional

BOWLS
2 to 3 large (8-inch [20-cm]) carrots, shaved into noodles

TOPPINGS
Smoked or roasted nuts, crushed

Fresh cilantro or basil, chopped

Crushed red pepper flakes

1 to 2 tbsp (6 to 12 g) capers

Olive oil

To make the creamy red pepper sauce, soak the cashews in purified water for at least 2 hours or up to 24 hours in the fridge. Drain, reserving ½ cup (120 ml) of the water for blending.

In a food processor, combine the soaked cashews, roasted red peppers, garlic, onion powder, salt, pepper, green onion, olive oil, lemon juice and mustard. Blend until a creamy sauce is formed. For a sauce thicker sauce, add a spoonful of coconut cream to the food processor mixture and blend well. For a thinner sauce, add a splash of almond milk or the reserved soaking water.

For the bowls, heat the carrot noodles in a large pan over medium heat for 30 to 45 seconds. Add the red pepper sauce, and stir to combine. Cook until the sauce and carrot noodles are mixed and warm, stirring gently.

Serve in 2 bowls. Top with the nuts, cilantro, red pepper flakes and capers. Drizzle with the olive oil.

Note: For a spicy sauce, add in 1 tablespoon (12 g) of crushed red pepper or Tabasco and cayenne pepper to the food processor, and blend well.

SPICY BEET POTATO SALAD BOWLS

I love this beet potato salad as a full meal in itself. Why? Because you just can't beat this flavor combo or the health benefits! Did you know that beets are actually healing foods? They are naturally high in anti-inflammatory properties, antioxidants, vitamins and minerals.

PREP TIME: 10 MINUTES • COOKING TIME: 6 MINUTES • SERVES: 2 TO 3

4 to 6 red potatoes, sliced and chopped

2 tbsp (30 ml) veggie broth or water

Fine sea salt or kosher salt, to taste

Pepper, to taste

2 cups (240 g) beets, sliced and cooked

3 tbsp (45 ml) olive oil, divided, plus more for topping

1 tsp minced garlic

2 green onions or ¼ to ⅓ cup (40 to 50 g) chopped red onion

½ tsp smoked paprika or cayenne

3 to 4 tbsp (45 to 60 ml) almond milk or coconut milk or cream

½ lemon, juiced

1 jalapeño, plus extra for topping

Handful of roasted, salted or smoked almonds, crushed

Lemon slices

Cilantro, for garnish

Vegan cheese or sour cream

Tabasco

In a microwave-safe bowl, combine the red potatoes with the broth. Microwave for 6 minutes until tender, but not overcooked. Pulse the potatoes in a blender or finely chop, then add a pinch of salt and pepper. Set aside in a large bowl.

In a blender or food processor, combine the beets, 2 tablespoons (30 ml) of olive oil, garlic, salt, pepper, green onions, paprika, almond milk and lemon juice. Blend until mixed but still chunky. Scrape the sides and pulse again. Taste and season with more salt and pepper if needed.

Add the beet mixture to the potatoes, mixing well. Add the chopped jalapeño and an additional 1 tablespoon (15 ml) of oil. Season with additional paprika, if desired.

Divide into 2 to 3 separate bowls. Top with the extra jalapeño slices, crushed smoked nuts, lemon slices and cilantro. Add the vegan cheese, season with salt and pepper, and drizzle with olive oil and Tabasco.

FAMILY-STYLE LARGE BOWLS

Who said family style needed plates? Personally, I think gathering around the table with a big bowl of food is more fun and exciting! Don't you?

When my husband used to train for triathlons, we often had people stay with us for training camps. Making family style bowls was perfect for feeding 3 to 5 people, and quick! Real food, real fuel and real good. Just check out the Baja Fish Taco Bowl (page 118) and see for yourself.

BAJA FISH TACO BOWL

This Baja Fish Taco Bowl is a family favorite! The red cabbage slaw provides your daily dose of vitamin C and vitamin K. The avocado crema sauce and fish add a boost of protein and omegas.

PREP TIME: 10 MINUTES • **COOKING TIME: 6 MINUTES** • **SERVES: 4 TO 6**

BAJA FISH
10 oz (285 g) cod or halibut

2 tbsp (30 ml) avocado oil, plus more for frying

½ to 1 tbsp (8 to 15 ml) chili sauce or Sriracha

1 tbsp (11 g) rice flour or potato flour

Fresh lime juice

Sea salt, to taste

Pepper, to taste

SAUCE
1 green onion

2 cloves garlic

½ avocado

1 red chili pepper, stem cut off

¼ cup (45 ml) avocado or olive oil

¼ tsp cumin

¼ tsp chili powder

1 handful fresh cilantro

1 tbsp (15 ml) lime juice

LA CREMA TOPPING
½ avocado

¼ cup (55 g) Paleo mayo or olive oil–based mayo

2 tbsp (30 ml) olive or avocado oil

1 tbsp (15 ml) lime juice

Pinch of garlic powder

½ green onion

1 tsp chili powder, optional

BOWLS
½ head cabbage

Handful of sliced red pepper (such as cayenne) or jalapeño

Crumbled Cotija cheese

Pepita seeds

Gluten-free or corn tortillas, or large lettuce leaves, for serving

To make the Baja fish, clean and dry the fish, then cut into bite-size pieces, around ¾-inch (19-mm) wide. In a small bowl, place the oil and chili sauce. In another bowl, place the flour.

Dip the fish in the oil and chili sauce, then the flour. In a sauté pan, place half of the portion of fish with ½ tablespoon (8 ml) of oil and cook over medium-high heat. Turn the fish while cooking for 3 to 6 minutes, or until it is cooked through and golden. Repeat with the other half. After cooking, drain the fish on a layer of paper towels.

Add a squeeze of fresh lime juice, and sea salt and pepper to taste to the fish. Set aside while you prepare the rest of the bowl.

For the sauce, combine the green onion, garlic, avocado, pepper, oil, cumin, chili powder, cilantro, lime juice, salt and pepper in a blender. Blend well. Set aside in a small bowl.

For the la crema topping, combine the avocado, mayo, oil, lime juice, garlic powder, green onion, optional chili pepper, salt and pepper in a blender. Blend until creamy and set aside.

For the bowls, cut the cabbage into quarters or smaller and set aside a large leaf to line the bowl. Place the cabbage in a food processor and pulse until a riced slaw is formed. Place the cabbage in a large bowl and squeeze out all of the extra water. Pat dry with a paper towel. Pour the sauce over the cabbage and mix well to combine.

To arrange the family-style bowl, place a large cabbage leaf at the bottom of the bowl. Add the cabbage rice and top with the Baja fish. Top with red pepper and drizzle with the la crema topping. Sprinkle with Cotija cheese and pepita seeds, and season with salt and pepper to taste. Serve with tortillas on the side for scooping.

TEX MEX BURRITO BOWL

One big bowl of all your burrito favorites! This is such a fun family-style bowl because you can customize it as you like with black beans, rice, avocado, protein and extra veggies. No one will know it's actually healthy and gluten-free. Just gather around the table and dive right in!

PREP TIME: 10 MINUTES • COOKING TIME: 20 MINUTES • SERVES: 4

SALSA
⅓ cup (55 g) cherry tomatoes

⅓ cup (50 g) yellow onion, chopped

2 cloves garlic

1 red jalapeño or serrano (remove seeds for less spice)

1 tsp cumin

Fine sea salt or kosher salt, to taste

Pepper, to taste

BEEF FILLING
8 to 10 oz (230 to 285 g) lean steak

1 tsp chili powder

1 tbsp (15 ml) avocado oil or clarified butter, plus more for topping

BOWL
2 cups (320 g) cooked rice

1 cup (200 g) cooked black beans

½ bell pepper, sliced

2 to 3 cups (80 to 120 g) chopped greens

½ avocado

¼ cup (30 g) sour cream

Fresh cilantro

Sliced lime

Tabasco, optional

Grated natural cheese, for topping

2 (10-inch [25-cm]) gluten-free tortillas

To make the salsa, combine the cherry tomatoes, onion, garlic, jalapeño, cumin, salt and pepper in a food processor. Blend until a salsa-like texture is formed and place in a medium bowl. Set aside.

Preheat the oven to 400°F (204°C).

For the beef filling, rub the steak with chili powder, salt, pepper and avocado oil. Bake for 20 minutes on a baking sheet. Remove the excess fat, then shred or chop the steak.

For the bowl, place the rice in a large serving bowl, followed by the beans and beef.

Layer on the bell pepper, chopped greens, avocado, salsa and sour cream. Top with the cilantro and a squeeze of lime. Drizzle with avocado oil and Tabasco, if desired. Sprinkle with grated natural cheese and season with salt and pepper.

Serve with lightly baked gluten-free tortillas on the side to scoop up the fillings.

SWEET AND SOUR HAM PASTA BOWL

Sweet, sour and oh so delicious! This is one of those "repurpose your leftovers" kind of meals. All you need are some gluten-free pantry staples, like leftover smoked or honey ham, and fresh pineapple! Fresh pineapple contains an enzyme that helps break down protein during digestion. This bowl is sure to feed and nourish a hungry family.

PREP TIME: 10 MINUTES • COOKING TIME: 9 TO 12 MINUTES • SERVES: 6

SAUCE

½ cup (120 ml) pineapple juice

2 to 3 tbsp (30 to 45 ml) chili sauce

1 tbsp (12 g) coconut or raw sugar

1 tbsp (11 g) tapioca or potato starch

3 tsp (15 ml) apple cider or rice vinegar

1 tsp mustard

BOWL

1 tbsp (15 ml) avocado or sesame oil

½ cup (75 g) chopped onion

1 tsp minced garlic

2 cups (80 g) chopped greens or broccoli

2 cups (300 g) diced smoked ham

1 cup (225 g) diced pineapple

¼ tsp fine sea salt or kosher salt

¼ tsp pepper

10 to 12 oz (285 to 340 g) gluten-free pasta, cooked (see note)

Red chili pepper flakes

Fresh cilantro

Parmesan cheese, optional

To make the sauce, combine the pineapple juice, chili sauce, coconut sugar, tapioca, vinegar and mustard in a blender. Blend well.

For the bowls, heat the oil in a large sauté pan over medium heat. Add the onion and garlic, cooking until the onions are translucent, about 2 minutes. Add the chopped greens, cooking until wilted, another 1 to 2 minutes. Add the smoked ham, pineapple, salt and pepper. Cook for 3 to 4 minutes, then add the cooked pasta and sauce to the pan. Stir to combine and cook for another 3 to 4 minutes.

Serve from one large bowl or divide equally among serving bowls. Top with red chili flakes and fresh cilantro. Drizzle with any extra sauce left in the pan, and sprinkle with Parmesan, if desired.

Note: Quinoa, brown rice or other gluten-free pasta works best.

STICKY MONGOLIAN BEEF BROCCOLI RICE BOWLS

Sticky Mongolian Beef Broccoli Rice Bowls are easy to cook in just 30 minutes. Light and full of garlic and ginger flavors, this Asian-inspired grain-free recipe is perfect for busy weeknights.

PREP TIME: 1 HOUR, 10 MINUTES • COOKING TIME: 20 MINUTES • SERVES: 3 TO 4

MONGOLIAN SAUCE

¼ to ⅓ cup (60 to 80 ml) gluten-free tamari or soy sauce

⅓ cup (80 ml) chicken broth or water

¼ cup (50 g) coconut sugar (see notes)

1 tbsp (15 ml) avocado oil or sesame oil

1 tsp minced garlic

½ tsp grated ginger

BOWLS

1 lb (454 g) beef sirloin (sliced thin, ¼- to ⅓-inch [6- to 8-mm] thick

1 tsp avocado or sesame oil, plus ⅓ cup (80 ml) for frying

1 tsp arrowroot starch or potato starch plus ¼ cup (45 g) more (see notes)

1 head broccoli

1 tbsp (15 ml) broth or water

Salt

Pepper

2 green onions, sliced

1 tsp red pepper flakes

Sesame seeds, for garnish

Fresh cilantro, for garnish

To make the Mongolian sauce, whisk together the tamari, broth and coconut sugar in a small bowl. Set aside. In a small saucepan, add the oil, garlic and grated ginger. Stir fry until fragrant, about 2 to 3 minutes. Add the tamari mixture to the saucepan, bring to a boil, then reduce heat and simmer on low until thickened, about 10 minutes.

For the bowls, toss the beef in 1 teaspoon of oil and then 1 teaspoon of starch. Place in a bowl or Ziploc bag with the Mongolian sauce and marinate in the fridge for 10 minutes or up to 1 hour.

Once marinated, lightly coat the beef strips in an extra ¼ cup (45 g) of arrowroot starch. Heat a large skillet with ⅓ cup (80 ml) of oil, then place the beef strips in the pan. Fry in the oil for about 1 minute on each side, browning each steak strip. Set the beef strips on a paper-towel-lined plate and drain the oil from the pan. Place the beef strips back in the pan with the Mongolian sauce. Reduce the heat, then cook the meat for 1 minute, stirring to coat. Remove from the heat and set aside.

Cut the broccoli head into 3 or 4 parts. Working in batches, process in a blender or food processor until a riced texture is achieved. Place in a large microwave-safe bowl. Add the broth, and salt and pepper to taste. Lightly steam in the microwave for 45 seconds to 1 minute.

Divide the broccoli rice between each of the bowls. Add the beef to each bowl and drizzle the sauce on top.

Top with the green onions and red pepper flakes. Garnish with the sesame seeds and cilantro.

Notes: For an extra-spicy bowl, add 1 sliced red Thai pepper to your sauce or to the beef when frying.

The sauce also works great with coconut palm sugar or raw turbinado sugar. Honey will work in place of coconut sugar, but the beef will be stickier.

For a Paleo option, substitute cornstarch for the arrowroot starch.

SPANISH SLOW COOKER SHRIMP QUINOA BOWLS

Can you tell how much I love Spanish flavors? These bowls start out as a one-pot wonder that slow-cooks to perfection. They're balanced in protein, ancient grains, vegetables and smoky spices! You'll love that these bowls are easy to prep and freezer friendly, too!

PREP TIME: 10 MINUTES ◦ **COOKING TIME: 2½ TO 3½ HOURS** ◦ **SERVES: 3 TO 4**

1 cup (170 g) quinoa, rinsed

2 cups (480 ml) water or broth

1 tbsp (15 ml) olive oil

1 (14-oz [400-g]) can fire-roasted tomatoes, drained

2 tbsp (30 ml) honey

1 tbsp (15 ml) lime juice

½ tsp cayenne pepper

1 tbsp (15 ml) tamari or gluten-free Worcestershire sauce

½ tsp smoked paprika

1 tsp onion powder

1 tsp dried coriander

1 cup (160 g) frozen spinach

6 to 10 oz (170 to 285 g) peeled shrimp (tail off), frozen

1 cup (50 g) green onion, chopped

Crumbled goat cheese or Parmesan

Cayenne pepper

Fresh herbs such as oregano or parsley

Salt

Pepper

In a slow cooker, add the quinoa, water, olive oil, tomatoes, honey, lime juice, cayenne, tamari, paprika, onion powder, coriander, spinach and frozen shrimp. Mix until combined.

Cook on high heat for 2 to 2½ hours or on low for 3 to 3½ hours. If using fresh shrimp, add them for the last hour of cooking. Check for doneness after an hour or 90 minutes to see the progress of the shrimp and quinoa.

Place in 1 large serving bowl or 2 to 3 separate bowls once cooled. Top with the green onion, a sprinkle of crumbled goat cheese, a pinch of cayenne pepper and fresh herbs. Season with salt and pepper to taste.

MOJO SALMON BOWLS

Winner, winner, let's spice up dinner! This is one serious dinner bowl with a nutritious punch—salmon, black beans, grilled pineapple, plantains and avocado. This Cuban-inspired meal is packed with fiber, healthy fats, resistant starches, omegas and immunity-boosting superfruit. Best of all, it takes only 30 minutes to make!

PREP TIME: 20 MINUTES • COOKING TIME: 20 TO 25 MINUTES • SERVES: 3 TO 4

MOJO SAUCE
½ cup (120 ml) orange juice
½ tsp cumin
½ tsp dried oregano
¼ tsp or more fine sea salt or kosher salt
⅛ tsp pepper
1 to 2 tbsp (15 to 30 ml) lime juice
2 tbsp (5 g) chopped fresh cilantro
1 tsp minced garlic
¼ cup (60 ml) olive oil

BOWLS
8 to 10 oz (230 to 285 g) wild-caught salmon fillets
2 tsp (10 ml) avocado or olive oil
4 to 5 pineapple slices, ½-inch (1-cm) thick
1 ripe plantain, sliced
1 to 1½ cups (160 to 240 g) white rice, cooked
1 avocado
1 tomato, sliced
5 cups (900 g) lightly steamed greens
15 oz (425 g) cooked black beans
1 tbsp (15 ml) fresh lime juice

TOPPINGS
Lime wedge
1 green onion, white portion only, chopped
Handful of fresh cilantro
1 tbsp (2 g) crushed red pepper flakes
1 sliced jalapeño, optional
Paprika or cayenne pepper, optional

To make the mojo sauce, whisk together the orange juice, cumin, oregano, salt, pepper, lime juice, cilantro, garlic and olive oil. Pour the mojo sauce over the salmon fillets, reserving ¼ cup (60 ml). Marinate in the fridge for 10 minutes.

Preheat the oven to 415°F (212°C). Preheat a grill or indoor grill top.

For the bowls, bake the salmon on a baking sheet for 10 to 12 minutes. Set aside.

Add the oil to the pineapple and plantain, and grill over medium-high heat for 10 minutes, flipping halfway through. Add 2 to 3 tablespoons (30 to 45 ml) of the reserved marinade on top of the pineapples in the last few minutes of cooking.

Place the rice in 1 large serving bowl or 3 to 4 separate bowls. Top with the salmon, grilled pineapple and plantains, avocado, tomato, steamed greens and black beans. Add a squeeze of fresh lime. Season with salt and pepper. Top with the green onion, cilantro, crushed red pepper flakes and jalapeño, if desired.

Sprinkle the bowls with a pinch of paprika, if desired.

DECONSTRUCTED STUFFED BELL PEPPER BOWL

I will confess, I always loved stuffed peppers but thought the whole process took too long, and they were hard to eat. That's why I made this Deconstructed Stuffed Bell Pepper Bowl: family friendly, easy to make, easy to clean up and easy to devour! The combo of lean beef and bell peppers make for one iron-boosting and antioxidant-rich bowl.

PREP TIME: 5 TO 10 MINUTES • **COOKING TIME: 19 TO 22 MINUTES** • **SERVES: 4 TO 5**

BEEF
1 tsp olive oil

1 lb (455 g) lean ground beef

2 tsp (7 g) minced garlic

1 cup (150 g) chopped onion

1 cup (150 g) chopped bell pepper

½ to 1 tsp red pepper flakes or Italian seasoning

Fine sea salt or kosher salt, to taste

Pepper, to taste

8 oz (230 g) tomato sauce

2 tsp (10 ml) gluten-free Worcestershire sauce or tamari

BOWL
3 cups (555 g) cooked quinoa

3 cups (540 g) lightly steamed spinach

1 bell pepper, sliced thin

Handful of fresh torn cilantro

1 green onion, chopped

Handful of sliced cherry tomatoes

Kefir yogurt cheese or sour cream, optional, for topping

Red pepper flakes, hot sauce or Tabasco, optional, for topping

Lemon slices, for garnish

To make the beef, heat the oil in a large skillet over medium heat. Add the ground beef and cook until no longer pink, about 7 to 10 minutes. Drain off any extra fat. Add the garlic and onion, cooking for 2 minutes until fragrant. Add the chopped bell pepper, red pepper flakes, salt and pepper, cooking for 5 minutes. Add the tomato sauce and Worcestershire sauce, and cook until bubbly, about 5 more minutes.

For the bowl, spoon the quinoa into a large bowl, followed by the spinach. Add in the ground beef mixture, and top with the sliced bell pepper, cilantro, green onion and cherry tomatoes. Season with salt and pepper to taste. Add a dollop of kefir yogurt cheese and red pepper flakes, if desired, and garnish with sliced lemon.

Serve in one large bowl or in individual bowls.

MACRO PICNIC SALAD BOWL

Seasonal vegetables, roasted chickpeas, chicken, potatoes and a simple homemade yogurt dressing make this a perfectly balanced macronutrient lunch or dinner.

PREP TIME: 10 MINUTES ◦ **COOKING TIME: 15 MINUTES** ◦ **SERVES: 5**

CREAMY POPPY YOGURT DRESSING
5 oz (142 g) plain yogurt

¼ cup (60 ml) olive oil

1 tbsp (15 ml) lemon juice

2 tbsp (30 ml) red wine vinegar

2 to 3 tbsp (30 to 45 ml) honey

1 to 2 tbsp (10 to 20 g) poppy seeds or sesame seeds

Pinch of fine sea salt or kosher salt

Pepper

½ tsp ground ginger

BOWL
1 medium sweet or Russet potato, spiralized or julienne cut

2 tsp (10 ml) oil

1 summer squash or zucchini, spiralized or julienne cut

3 cups (555 g) cooked quinoa

2 cups (80 g) mixed salad greens

6 oz (170 g) grilled or roasted chicken (skin removed), sliced

1 cup (200 g) roasted salted chickpeas or roasted nuts of choice

2 cups (310 g) Brussels sprouts, chopped

1 mandarin orange, sliced 1-inch (2.5-cm) thick

Fresh chopped cilantro, for topping

2 cups (100 g) broccoli or alfalfa sprouts

1 green onion, chopped

Poppy seeds or more sesame seeds, for garnish

Fresh lemon or lime wedge

To make the dressing, whisk together the yogurt, olive oil, lemon juice, honey, poppy seeds, salt, pepper and ginger together in a bowl. Transfer to an airtight container and store in the fridge until ready to use.

For the bowl, cook the potato noodles in a large skillet with the oil. Toss well. Let them cook on medium-high heat for 7 to 9 minutes, or until tender. Transfer the noodles to a serving bowl. Alternatively, bake the potato noodles on a greased baking tray in a 400°F (204°C) oven for 10 to 15 minutes. Set aside to cool.

Press the spiralized zucchini noodles with a paper towel to remove the excess water.

In a large bowl, layer the salad starting with the potato noodles. Add the zucchini noodles, then the quinoa. Surround the quinoa with greens, working your way all the way around. On top of the greens, layer the chicken, chickpeas and chopped Brussels sprouts.

Top the salad with the orange slices, cilantro, broccoli sprouts and green onion. Season with salt and pepper, and sprinkle the poppy seeds on top. Add a squeeze of lemon and drizzle the dressing on top before serving.

Note: Try mixing Parmesan crumbles into the potato salad for extra flavor.

COCONUT CURRIED PARSNIP RISOTTO BOWLS

Parsnips seem to be a forgotten vegetable these days. Yet, they are so delicious and nutritious: packed with fiber, folate, potassium and more. Plus, they make a great risotto substitute. This bowl is subtly spicy, nutty and perfectly sweet, just like me!

PREP TIME: 10 MINUTES • COOKING TIME: 8 TO 9 MINUTES • SERVES: 4 TO 5

RISOTTO

3 large parsnips, diced

1 tbsp (15 ml) olive oil or avocado oil

1 cup (150 g) chopped onion

1 tsp minced garlic

¼ tsp fine sea salt or kosher salt, plus more to taste

Pepper

½ cup (120 ml) coconut drinking milk

1 tbsp (15 g) red curry paste

¼ cup (60 ml) vegetable broth

½ tsp turmeric powder or curry powder

1 cup (150 g) green peas (fresh or frozen)

1 cup (40 g) spinach or kale (whole leaves or chopped)

TOPPINGS

Handful of fresh cilantro

Grated Parmesan cheese, optional

1 cup (200 g) roasted chickpeas (see notes)

Chili pepper flakes

Garlic powder

Lemon wedges

Olive oil

To make the risotto, add the parsnip pieces into a food processor and process until riced. Place in a large bowl and set aside.

Heat the oil in a skillet over medium heat. Add the onion, garlic, salt and pepper, and sauté until fragrant, about 2 minutes. Add the coconut milk and red curry paste, stirring until creamy, 1 to 2 minutes. Add the parsnips and continue cooking a few more minutes. Add the broth, turmeric, peas and spinach. Cover and cook over medium-low heat for 5 more minutes, or until the vegetables are cooked through. Place in a large serving bowl.

For the bowls, divide the parsnip risotto evenly among serving bowls. Top with the cilantro, Parmesan, roasted chickpeas and chili pepper flakes. Season with salt, pepper and garlic powder. Add a squeeze of lemon and a drizzle of olive oil over the top.

This dish may be served family style in 1 large bowl or divided into individual bowls.

Notes: Omit the Parmesan cheese if you want a vegan version.

For non-vegans, 6 ounces (170 g) cooked gluten-free chicken sausage maybe added for extra protein.

ANDALUCÍAN CAULIFLOWER RICE SALAD BOWL

Traditional Spanish Andalucían salad uses white rice as the base, and many other tangy and refreshing ingredients. This recipe exhibits those same flavor components, but lightens up the carbohydrates by replacing the rice with cauliflower rice. Loaded with prebiotic fibers and healthy fats to keep you and your family fueled and nourished—plus, there's no cooking needed!

PREP TIME: 10 TO 30 MINUTES · COOKING TIME: 0 MINUTES · SERVES: 3 TO 4

1 small head cauliflower

⅓ cup (60 g) diced pimentos

⅓ cup (60 g) diced marinated green olives

6 marinated artichoke hearts, chopped

⅓ cup (50 g) pepitas

¼ to ⅓ cup (10 to 14 g) cilantro, finely chopped, plus extra for topping

Fine sea salt or kosher salt

Pepper

¼ to ½ tsp garlic powder

Sliced green or red jalapeño

Crumbled feta or Parmesan cheese, optional

Olive oil

Red wine vinegar

Cut the cauliflower head into 3 to 4 parts. Working in batches, process in a blender or food processor until a riced texture is achieved. Place in a large bowl.

Toss the rice with the pimentos, green olives, artichoke hearts, pepitas, cilantro, salt, pepper and garlic powder. Let the mixture sit in the fridge to marinate, about 10 to 20 minutes, to enhance the flavor, or serve right away.

Top with the cilantro, jalapeño and feta cheese, if desired. Drizzle with the olive oil and red wine vinegar.

Serve straight from the bowl.

Note: To add protein, toss in cooked chickpeas, chicken, shrimp or black beans.

DUKKAH ROASTED VEGGIE PILAF BOWL

Back in 2005, I had the privilege of working at an orphanage in Africa. It was life changing. The people were so giving and kind. Each night we'd get a simple meal of vegetables and spices or sauces, sometimes with meat, but most of the time without. Regardless, those few ingredients created a flavorful, nourishing meal. Just like this Dukkah Roasted Veggie Pilaf Bowl. Inspired by simple African spices and the simplest of vegetables, I think you'll love it! Do me a favor though, slow down and savor each bite!

PREP TIME: 8 MINUTES • COOKING TIME: 22 MINUTES • SERVES: 5

4 cups (920 g) finely chopped cauliflower

2 cups (135 g) sliced mushrooms

1 cup (150 g) pearl onions, peeled and sliced in half

1 cup (160 g) sliced cherry tomatoes

1 cup (200 g) chickpeas, optional

⅓ cup (80 ml) olive oil

1 tbsp (8 g) or more dukkah seasoning (see notes)

1 cup (40 g) chopped spinach greens or Brussels sprouts

¼ cup (40 g) pepitas

¼ tsp fine sea salt or kosher salt

¼ tsp black pepper, or to taste

½ tsp garlic powder

2 cups (340 g) quinoa

Broth

TOPPINGS
Sprouts

⅔ cup (80 g) sliced fresh radish, optional

Fresh lemon

Parmesan shavings, optional (see notes)

Creamy yogurt dressing or nondairy dressing of choice

Preheat the oven to 425°F (218°C).

In a large bowl, toss the cauliflower, mushrooms, onions, tomatoes and chickpeas in olive oil and dukkah seasoning. Spread the mixture on large baking sheet, and add the greens and pepitas. Season with salt, pepper and garlic powder.

Roast the vegetables for 15 to 18 minutes or until the cauliflower is cooked through. Remove from the oven and set aside.

Cook the quinoa according to package directions, replacing the water with broth to create a pilaf. Once cooked, fluff and set aside.

To serve, layer a large serving bowl with the quinoa, then add the roasted vegetables. Top with the sprouts, sliced radish, a squeeze of lemon, Parmesan and a dollop of yogurt for dressing. Season with salt and pepper to taste. It can be tossed together or served as-is.

Notes: If you don't have dukkah spice, simply replace 1 tablespoon of dukkah seasoning with a mixture of 1 teaspoon of cumin, 1 teaspoon of sesame seeds, ½ teaspoon of coriander seeds, ¼ teaspoon of salt, ¼ teaspoon of pepper and 1 teaspoon of finely crushed toasted nuts, such as hazelnuts.

For Paleo and vegan options, omit the Parmesan and yogurt topping, and use a nondairy-based dressing of choice.

FARMERS MARKET SUMMER STEW BOWLS

The most flavorful and nutrient-dense vegetables are the ones around you—locally sourced and in season. This summer stew is a great way to utilize all of those seasonal vegetables. Hearty, yet still light in taste, this makes a great dish for summer. These stew bowls make for easy meal prep, so go ahead, make a double batch!

PREP TIME: 10 MINUTES • COOKING TIME: 30 MINUTES • SERVES: 6

2 tbsp (30 ml) olive oil or clarified butter, divided

12 oz (340 g) gluten-free chicken sausage or chorizo, sliced

1 small yellow squash, sliced

⅔ cup (100 g) chopped red onion

2 cups (360 g) steamed kale

1 large celery stalk, about ½ cup (75 g) chopped

1 tsp minced garlic (2 large cloves garlic)

½ tsp fine sea salt or kosher salt, or to taste

½ tsp pepper, or to taste

⅔ cup (155 ml) chicken or vegetable broth

20- to 25-oz (around 2½ to 3 cups [500 to 600 g]) canned chickpeas or canned white beans, drained

2 (8-oz [230-g]) cans stewed plum tomatoes

3 tbsp (50 g) tomato sauce

3 thyme sprigs

½ tsp dried oregano

5 large asparagus spears, shaved (see note)

Fresh parsley, for garnish

½ cup (90 g) grated Parmesan cheese, for topping

Hard-boiled or fried eggs to top each serving, optional

In a large skillet, heat 1 tablespoon (15 ml) of olive oil. Add the chicken sausage, cooking about 5 to 7 minutes or until browned on each side. If using pre-cooked sausage, heat through. Remove from the pan.

Add the remaining tablespoon (15 ml) of oil to the skillet, then add the yellow squash, red onion, kale, celery, garlic, salt and pepper. Sauté until fragrant, about 2 minutes. Add the sausage, broth, chickpeas, tomatoes and tomato sauce, and bring to a boil. Add the thyme and oregano. Reduce and simmer 10 to 20 minutes, or until the flavors combine and the veggies are cooked. Taste and add more seasoning if needed.

Add the asparagus shavings to a microwave-safe bowl with 1 tablespoon (15 ml) of water and microwave for 30 to 45 seconds, or until slightly steamed. Alternatively, place the shavings in with the stew the last 5 minutes of cooking.

Spoon the stew into bowls, making sure to include both the broth and veggies, and add the steamed asparagus ribbons on top. Garnish with the fresh parsley and sprinkle with Parmesan. Season with salt and pepper. Top each bowl with a cooked egg, if desired.

Note: Shave the asparagus spears in ribbons using a peeler. Start at the tip of the asparagus spear and peel down toward the stem. I like to add the steamed asparagus ribbons last, so they don't overcook.

FIRECRACKER TURKEY RICE BOWL

These bowls literally burst with flavor. I love making them for an easy meal-prep recipe or quick dinner. The firecracker sauce can be made spicy or creamy—you choose! Either way, you'll love this balanced meal.

PREP TIME: 10 MINUTES · COOKING TIME: 20 MINUTES · SERVES: 4 TO 5

FIRECRACKER SAUCE

3 oz (85 g) dried red peppers or sun-dried tomatoes

⅓ cup (80 ml) tomato sauce

2 tsp (1 g) crushed red pepper flakes (omit if you want it less spicy)

1 tsp minced garlic

Handful of spinach leaves

¼ cup (60 ml) olive oil

Lemon juice

Fine sea salt or kosher salt

Pepper

BOWLS

2 cups (420 g) white rice

3 cups (710 ml) broth, divided

1 cup (175 g) broccoli, chopped or florets

1 tbsp + 2 tsp (25 ml) avocado, olive or coconut oil, divided

⅓ cup (50 g) chopped onion

1 lb (455 g) ground lean turkey

½ tsp cumin

¼ to ½ tsp paprika, smoked or regular

Pinch of garlic salt

Tabasco or chili sauce

Fresh cilantro or herb of choice

Diced red pepper

To make the firecracker sauce, combine the red peppers, tomato sauce, crushed red pepper flakes, garlic, spinach, olive oil, lemon juice, salt and pepper in a food processor. Blend until a thick paste is formed. Add more oil or even low-sodium tamari if you want to thin it out.

For the bowls, cook the rice in a medium pot according to the package directions, replacing the water with broth. Once cooked, fluff and place in a large bowl.

In a food processor, add the broccoli and process until a rice is formed. Remove and mix with cooked white rice.

In a large pan, heat 2 teaspoons (10 ml) of oil. Add the onion and cook until translucent, about 2 minutes. Add the ground turkey and cook until browned, 3 to 4 minutes. Drain off any excess fat. Add the cumin and salt and pepper to taste.

Mix well and add ½ to ⅔ cup (118 to 155 ml) of broth, 1 tablespoon (15 ml) of oil, ½ teaspoon of paprika and garlic salt, and mix again. Add the firecracker sauce and mix to combine. Cook over medium heat until cooked through, about 5 minutes, stirring a few times while cooking.

Place the broccoli and rice mixture in a large serving bowl. Add the ground turkey mixture. Drizzle with Tabasco or chili sauce. Top with the cilantro and diced red pepper.

This dish may be served family style in one large bowl or divided into individual bowls.

Note: Depending on how many spinach leaves you use, your firecracker sauce can turn out more of a red or green color. Using sun-dried peppers creates a fiery red sauce. Sun-dried tomatoes make a milder, yet flavorful, firecracker sauce.

SOUTHERN CAESAR SALAD POWER BOWL

Southerners know their vegetables! I'm a Southerner—I can say that, which is why I love this Southern style Caesar salad with mustard greens, black-eyed peas and lima beans. High in fiber, rich in vitamin A, vitamin K, calcium and plant-based iron.

PREP TIME: 10 MINUTES • COOKING TIME: 10 MINUTES • SERVES: 3

CAESAR DRESSING

1 egg yolk

½ tbsp (8 ml) honey mustard

3 to 4 tbsp (45 to 60 ml) olive oil or avocado oil

¼ tsp fine sea salt or kosher salt, to taste

¼ tsp pepper, to taste

½ to 1 tsp anchovy paste (see note)

1 to 2 tsp (4 to 7 g) minced garlic

1 tbsp (15 ml) lemon juice

BOWL

1 tsp olive or avocado oil, or clarified butter

½ cup (75 g) chopped onion (white or red)

5 to 6 cups (200 to 245 g) chopped mustard greens

1 cup (150 g) green peas, black-eyed peas or lima beans, canned or cooked and drained

Lemon wedge

¼ tsp paprika

½ cup (30 g) toasted gluten-free bread crumbs

1 cup (160 g) cherry tomatoes, chopped

½ cup (115 g) zucchini, sliced

TOPPINGS

Grated Parmesan cheese, optional

Sprouts

Garlic powder, to taste

Crushed red pepper flakes, optional

Garlic powder, optional

Lemon wedges

Tabasco

To make the Caesar dressing, whisk together the egg yolk, honey mustard, oil, salt, pepper, anchovy paste, garlic and lemon juice in a medium bowl until creamy.

For the bowl, heat the oil in a sauté pan over medium to medium-high heat. Add the onion and stir-fry until fragrant. Add the mustard greens, peas, a splash of lemon, paprika and sea salt. Toss, cover and steam for 3 to 5 minutes.

Place the steamed greens and peas in a large bowl. Add the toasted gluten-free bread crumbs, cherry tomatoes and zucchini. Toss with the Caesar dressing. Top with the grated Parmesan if desired and sprouts. Season with salt, pepper and garlic powder to taste. Sprinkle with the crushed red pepper flakes, if desired, then drizzle with the lemon and Tabasco.

Serve from one large bowl.

Note: For a fish-free version of anchovy paste, add a pinch of salt or capers mashed with garlic to the dressing.

CAJUN FRIED RICE GRAIN BOWLS

Don't let the fried part of this bowl fool you. These fried rice bowls are perfectly healthy and delicious! A mix of ancient grains lightly fried with eggs, Cajun chicken sausage and vegetables. Simple ingredients with bold flavors.

PREP TIME: 10 MINUTES • COOKING TIME: 20 MINUTES • SERVES: 2 TO 3

2 cups (420 g) mixed gluten-free grains (see notes)

1 to 2 tbsp (15 to 30 ml) olive oil

⅓ cup (50 g) chopped onion

1 tsp minced garlic (1 large clove or 2 small)

¼ tsp fine sea salt or kosher salt

¼ tsp pepper

¼ tsp paprika

½ tsp Creole spice mix (or any other Cajun spice mix with cayenne, red pepper and garlic)

3 oz (85 g) chopped gluten-free chicken or turkey sausage (see notes)

⅓ cup (80 ml) vegetable broth

¼ cup (60 ml) tomato sauce or spicy chili sauce

⅔ cup (100 g) celery, chopped

⅔ cup (100 g) red or green bell pepper, chopped

2 eggs

Parsley, for garnish

Crushed red pepper flakes

Cayenne pepper, optional

Tabasco, optional, for garnish

Cooked, chopped nitrate-free bacon or turkey bacon, optional, for garnish

Cook the grains according to the package directions. Once cooked, place in a large bowl and set aside.

In a large skillet or wok, heat the oil and sauté the chopped onion and garlic until fragrant, about 1 to 2 minutes. Add in the mixed grains, salt, pepper, paprika and Creole spices, mixing together.

Add the chicken sausage to the pan and cook the sausage and grains over medium heat until cooked through, 5 to 7 minutes until no longer pink. You can use precooked sausage for quicker cooking.

Evenly pour in the vegetable broth and tomato sauce into the pan. Then add the celery and bell pepper, and cook over medium heat for 2 to 3 minutes.

Whisk together 2 eggs and add to the pan with the sausage, grains and veggies. Stir fry until eggs are cooked through, 2 to 3 minutes.

Spoon the cooked mixture in a large serving bowl or 2 to 3 bowls. Add the parsley to garnish, and season with salt and pepper to taste. Sprinkle with the crushed red pepper flakes and extra cayenne, if desired.

For an extra kick, mix in a few teaspoons of Tabasco and top with chopped bacon, if desired, before serving.

Notes: A mix of leftover cooked, gluten-free grains can be used for this recipe, such as a mix of cooked quinoa and rice. I like to use a nutty grain like quinoa for texture and then another grain such as white rice for light flavor.

Be sure to use gluten-free chicken sausage or turkey sausage to keep this on the lighter side. You can use organic chicken sausage patties or links to make this dish casein-free.

CHOPPED SUPERFOOD POWER SALAD BOWL

When you think of superfoods, I hope color comes to mind. Yes, the most colorful fruit and vegetables are usually the richest in antioxidants. This chopped superfood salad is bursting with nourishment and immunity-boosting ingredients. Now, chop to it and let's eat!

PREP TIME: 10 MINUTES • **COOKING TIME: 0 MINUTES** • **SERVES: 3 TO 4**

3 cups (1 kg) Brussels sprouts, chopped or shaved

2 to 2½ cups (370 to 460 g) cooked quinoa

⅓ cup (55 g) smoked or roasted almonds, chopped

3 tbsp (10 g) diced green onions, green parts only

1½ cups (150 g) fresh raspberries

½ to ⅔ cup (170 to 225 g) chopped carrot

¼ cup (10 g) chopped fresh basil

½ small lemon, juiced

3 tbsp (45 ml) olive oil

Red wine vinegar or balsamic vinaigrette

¼ tsp fine sea salt or kosher salt, to taste

¼ tsp black pepper, to taste

Crumbled feta cheese, optional, for topping (see note)

In a large bowl, place the chopped Brussels sprouts and the cooked quinoa. Toss them together.

Add the almonds, green onions, raspberries, carrot, basil, lemon juice, olive oil, vinegar, salt and pepper to the bowl. Toss together gently and sprinkle with the feta cheese, if desired.

Serve from 1 large bowl.

Note: For a vegan option, do not add feta cheese.

HIPPIE GRAIN BOWLS

This bowl was inspired by my frequent visits to a vegetarian restaurant while living in Austin, the hippie Texas town. A healthy, vegetarian grain bowl that feeds the whole family—full of balanced macronutrients, vitamins, minerals and more!

PREP TIME: 10 • COOKING TIME: 15 TO 20 MINUTES • SERVES: 4 TO 5

2 cups (370 g) cooked tri-colored quinoa (plain quinoa may be substituted)

1 cup (160 g) cooked white rice or brown rice

Fine sea salt or kosher salt

2 tsp (10 ml) olive or avocado oil, plus extra for drizzle

½ cup (75 g) white or yellow onion, chopped

15 oz (425 g) cooked black beans or pinto beans, drained

1 tsp minced garlic

Pinch of cumin

Pinch of cayenne

Ground black pepper

1 large carrot

1 small zucchini

2 to 3 tbsp (20 to 30 g) chia, sunflower or flax seeds

Fresh chopped cilantro, for garnish

⅓ cup (40 g) organic sour cream or Greek yogurt (see note)

Olive oil

In a large bowl, mix the quinoa and rice together. Add a pinch of sea salt and set aside.

In a saucepan, heat the oil and sauté the diced onions for 2 minutes. Add the beans, garlic, cumin and cayenne, cooking until fragrant. Season with sea salt and black pepper.

Using a spiralizer, spiralize or ribbon-cut the carrot and zucchini.

Arrange the cooked quinoa and rice mixture in a large serving bowl. Top with the cooked beans and spiralized carrots and zucchini. Sprinkle the seeds on top and garnish with a handful of cilantro.

Top the bowl with the sour cream and drizzle with the extra olive oil. You may want to season with additional salt and pepper after you serve into individual bowls.

Note: For a vegan option, replace the sour cream with nondairy yogurt, or omit.

SWEET TOOTH BOWLS

Of course, I saved the best for last. DESSERT! I know what you're thinking: Um, don't most desserts come served in a bowl? Well, not all!

These decadent, but healthy, dessert bowls are made with simple ingredients, real food and you can eat them anytime. No guilt there.

I'd have to say my favorite is the Triple Berry Shortcake Bowl (page 154) or the Vanilla Cheesecake Bowls with Fruit (page 161). Dairy-free, flourless and oh-my-heavens, yum!

TRIPLE BERRY SHORTCAKE BOWLS

The best thing about these cake bowls is that they only take a few ingredients and not a lot of prep. In fact, the cake itself is made in a matter of minutes. Wheatless, dairy-free, Paleo and did I mention delicious? Oh yes, have your cake and eat it too!

PREP TIME: 24 HOURS • COOKING TIME: 10 TO 25 MINUTES • SERVES: 2 TO 3

COCONUT WHIP
1 (13.6-oz [403-ml]) can coconut cream
¼ cup (60 ml) maple syrup or honey
1 tsp vanilla extract

BOWLS
3 tbsp (20 g) almond flour (not almond meal)
1 tbsp (11 g) coconut flour
½ tsp baking powder
Pinch of fine sea salt or kosher salt
1 tbsp (15 ml) coconut oil, melted
3 tbsp (45 ml) almond or coconut milk
1 tsp vanilla extract
¼ tsp raspberry or strawberry extract, optional
¼ cup (40 g) diced strawberries
1 egg
Fresh berries, for topping
Honey (see note)
Powdered sugar, optional, for topping

To make the coconut whip, first chill the can of coconut cream for 24 hours in the fridge.

Place the solid portion of the coconut cream in a bowl or stand mixer, discard the liquid portion and beat until creamy. Add the maple syrup and vanilla extract. Beat again until a whip is formed.

For the bowls, only one large mug is needed if making in the microwave. If using the oven, use 2 ramekins and preheat the oven to 350°F (177°C). Spray the mug or ramekins with cooking spray.

Place the almond flour, coconut flour, baking powder and salt in the mug, and mix the ingredients to combine.

In a separate bowl, mix the oil, almond milk, vanilla extract and raspberry extract.

Add the wet ingredients to the dry flour mixture, stirring to thoroughly combine. Add the strawberries and egg, mixing until smooth batter is formed.

Microwave for 90 to 120 seconds, or bake for 20 to 25 minutes.

Divide the coconut whip into bowls. Slice or crumble the strawberry mug cake into pieces, then add the cake slices on top or on the side of the coconut whip for each bowl. Top with the fresh berries and drizzle with the honey. Dust with powdered sugar, if desired, and any extra cake crumbles you make have.

Note: Xylitol syrup or baking stevia can be used in place of the honey to reduce sugar intake.

WHIPPED RICOTTA AND HONEY-GLAZED PEARS BOWLS

Glazed pears and whipped ricotta make such a lovely combo. It reminds me of the holidays. I know ricotta can be used sweet or savory, but I prefer it lightly sweetened with honey, then whipped to create more volume, similar to a yogurt consistency. Enjoy this bowl as a lighter dessert or even a decadent breakfast. This dessert bowl is light in texture but very filling. A little goes a long way. It's perfect for the holidays!

PREP TIME: 10 MINUTES • COOKING TIME: 8 MINUTES • SERVES: 3

GLAZED PEARS
¼ cup (60 ml) honey

1 tsp vanilla

Pinch of cardamom

½ to 1 tbsp (8 to 15 ml) balsamic vinegar

1 to 2 small pears, thinly sliced and core removed

BOWLS
1¼ cups (155 g) ricotta cheese (see notes)

⅓ to ½ cup (80 to 120 ml) honey (see notes)

1 tsp vanilla

Pinch of cinnamon

1 tbsp (15 g) coconut cream or heavy cream

TOPPINGS
Chopped nuts

Gluten-free granola

Cinnamon

Coconut sugar

To make the glazed pears, whisk together the honey, vanilla, cardamom and balsamic vinegar. Place the pears in a nonstick pan over medium heat and pour the glaze over the pears, reserving 2 tablespoons (30 ml) for the topping. Cook for 7 to 8 minutes, flipping once until the pears are soft and coated in the glaze.

For the bowls, combine the ricotta cheese, honey, vanilla, cinnamon and coconut cream in a medium bowl or stand mixer. Beat until the ricotta is smooth and fluffy. Keep refrigerated until ready to use.

Divide the ricotta mixture evenly among serving bowls. Top with the glazed pears and drizzle with the reserved glaze. Sprinkle on the nuts, granola, cinnamon and a pinch of coconut sugar. Serve with a gluten-free waffle for a breakfast or brunch, or serve for dessert.

Notes: Ricotta packs in 7 grams of filling protein per serving and a good dose of calcium. For lower lactose, try whole milk, goat's milk or sheep's milk ricotta.

Start with ⅓ cup (80 ml) of honey and add more if desired. This will impact your sugar intake.

CREAMY CHOCOLATE STREUSEL BOWLS

I love how quick and easy these dessert bowls are. No flour needed for these faux streusel bowls—just coconut oil, cocoa, flaxseed and unrefined sugar. Real food ingredient-based desserts are the way to go. And I bet you already have all these items in your pantry. Perfect! The flaxseed adds a nutty crunch and boost of omega-3s!

PREP TIME: 10 MINUTES • COOKING TIME: 2 TO 3 MINUTES • SERVES: 1 TO 2

STREUSEL
1 tbsp (8 g) milled flaxseed

1 tsp coconut oil

1 tsp cocoa powder, plus more for topping

1 tsp coconut sugar

BOWLS
1 cup (245 g) Greek yogurt (see notes)

2 tsp (5 g) cocoa powder, plus more for topping

1 small banana

¼ tsp vanilla extract

Honey or stevia

1 tbsp (12 g) dark chocolate chips (see notes)

Melted dark chocolate, optional

To make the streusel, combine the flaxseed, coconut oil, cocoa powder and coconut sugar in a small sauté pan. Sauté for 2 to 3 minutes over medium heat, toasting and mixing until a crumble topping is formed. Place the crumble in a small bowl and set aside.

For the bowls, combine the yogurt, cocoa powder, banana, vanilla and honey in a blender. Blend until combined and pour the yogurt mixture in 1 large bowl or 2 small serving bowls. Top with the chocolate streusel and dark chocolate chips. Dust with the cocoa powder. Drizzle the melted dark chocolate on top, if desired.

Notes: For a vegan option, use nondairy vegan yogurt.

Enjoy Life Foods Brand has delicious vegan and Paleo friendly dark chocolate chips that are great for topping or melting.

For an extra-rich dessert option, add a scoop of whipped coconut cream (see page 154), frozen yogurt or even fried sliced banana.

VANILLA CHEESECAKE BOWLS WITH FRUIT

I have never been a huge cheesecake fan . . . until now. This vegan bowl version is to die for!
It's light in texture, yet still creamy. Definitely lick the bowl worthy. This bowl is rich in plant-based
healthy fats and naturally sweetened with fruit and maple syrup.

PREP TIME: 24 HOURS • COOKING TIME: 1 MINUTES OR LESS • SERVES: 3 TO 5

BOWLS

2 (13-oz [370-g]) cans coconut cream (not milk)

8 oz (230 g) dairy-free cream cheese (see note)

½ cup (100 g) coconut sugar or maple syrup

1 ripe banana

1 tsp vanilla extract

1 tsp lemon zest or ½ tsp lemon extract

QUICK CARAMEL SAUCE

3 tbsp (45 ml) coconut sugar or maple syrup

¼ cup (60 ml) coconut milk (liquid)

TOPPINGS

Sliced fresh fruit

Crushed toasted nuts

Coconut shavings

Gluten-free granola

Cinnamon

For the bowls, chill the coconut cream can in the fridge for 24 hours and discard the liquid portion, then place the hardened cream portion in a stand mixer or bowl with a hand mixer. The cream should be a thick (similar to a cream cheese) texture. Beat until a fluffy frosting is formed. Add the vegan cream cheese, coconut sugar, banana, vanilla and lemon zest. Beat again on medium speed until thoroughly mixed. Taste and adjust for sweetness.

To make the quick caramel sauce, whisk the coconut sugar with the coconut milk in a small microwave-safe bowl. Microwave for 1 minute, or until the milk and sugar mixture are heated together to form a sweet sauce. This can be done on the stovetop as well by whisking the mixture together over medium-high heat until the sugar dissolves and thickens, about 5 minutes.

Pour the whipped mixture into serving bowls and drizzle with the quick caramel sauce. Top with the sliced fruit, nuts, coconut shavings, granola and a dash of cinnamon.

Note: I recommend the Daiya brand of vegan cream cheese. You can also use regular dairy cream cheese for a non-vegan alternative.

STICKY DATE CAKE YOGURT BOWLS

Did you know that soaking dates and blending them creates a sticky sweet paste? Oh, how I love nature's candy! All you need are a few minutes to bake the cake with the sticky date paste, then whip it together with yogurt and toppings. You'll never know this dessert bowl is actually good for you.

PREP TIME: 1 TO 2 HOURS • COOKING TIME: 2 TO 25 MINUTES • SERVES: 2

BOWLS

6 to 7 pitted dates

1½ cups (355 ml) purified water

1 tbsp (15 ml) honey

3 tbsp (20 g) almond flour (not meal)

1 tbsp (11 g) coconut flour

½ tsp baking powder

Pinch of fine sea salt or kosher salt

Pinch of cinnamon

1 tbsp (15 ml) coconut oil, melted

3 tbsp (45 ml) almond or coconut milk

½ tsp vanilla extract

1 egg

TOPPINGS

10 oz (285 g) yogurt or coconut yogurt, vanilla-flavored

1 banana, sliced

Crushed nuts or granola

Molasses

To make the bowls, soak the dates in purified water for 1 to 2 hours. Discard all of the water except 1 tablespoon (15 ml) after soaking. Blend the dates together with the honey to create a sticky paste. Set aside.

If making the cake in the microwave, only one large mug is needed. For the oven, use 2 ramekins and preheat the oven to 350°F (177°C). Spray the mug or ramekins with cooking spray.

Place the almond flour, coconut flour, baking powder, salt and cinnamon in the mug, and stir the ingredients to combine.

In a separate bowl, mix the oil, almond milk and vanilla.

Add the wet ingredients to the dry flour mixture, stirring to combine. Add the sticky date paste and egg, and mix until thoroughly combined.

Microwave for 90 to 120 seconds, or bake for 20 to 25 minutes.

Slice the cake into pieces and divide into serving bowls. Top with a dollop of yogurt, sliced banana, nuts and drizzle with molasses.

SPICED BAKED FRUIT BLISS BOWLS

This bliss bowl was actually inspired by one of my family's favorite holiday recipes. It takes simple fruit and tosses it with anti-inflammatory-rich spices and unrefined sugar, which allows the fruit to do its thing—shine with flavor and burst with sweetness. You can use just about any fruit, but I highly recommend fresh figs when they are in season. Oh, and I should mention that your house will smell amazing when you bake this. You will be hooked!

PREP TIME: 10 MINUTES • COOKING TIME: 30 MINUTES • SERVES: 3

6 fresh figs, sliced in half or quarters

2 to 3 stone fruit (apricots, plums or peaches), pitted, sliced in half or quarters

¼ cup (60 ml) melted butter or coconut oil (see note)

2 tbsp (30 ml) honey or maple syrup

1 to 2 tbsp (12 to 24 g) coconut sugar

½ tsp cinnamon

Pinch of nutmeg or pumpkin pie spice

¼ to ⅓ cup (40 to 55 g) slivered almonds or crushed nuts

Coconut cream or crème fraîche (see notes)

4 oz (115 g) pomegranate seeds

Cinnamon

Gluten-free granola, optional

Preheat the oven to 350°F (177°C). Grease or line a baking dish with parchment paper.

Place the figs and stone fruit facing up in the prepared baking dish.

In a small bowl, whisk together the butter, honey, coconut sugar, cinnamon and nutmeg. Pour the mixture over the fruit.

Bake for 15 minutes, then flip the fruit over. Bake for another 15 minutes. Sprinkle the almonds over the fruit for the last 10 to 15 minutes of baking.

Serve the bowls warm after dividing into 3 serving bowls. Top each bowl with a drizzle of coconut cream, pomegranate seeds, a dash of cinnamon and a sprinkle of gluten-free granola, if desired.

Notes: Coconut oil will give this bowl a different flavor and will harden at room temperature, but it works great too! Crème fraîche or regular cream may be used to drizzle, but is not vegan or Paleo friendly.

RUM RAISIN YOGURT OATMEAL CRISP BOWLS

Growing up, I used to love going to get ice cream after dinner with my dad. I would usually order rum raisin, and we would sit outside and enjoy our ice cream together. Of course, eating that every day wasn't the healthiest choice, but it did create a lot of fond memories. This rum raisin yogurt oatmeal crisp is definitely a wiser and healthier dessert choice today. Balanced with whole grains, calcium-rich yogurt and sun-dried raisins soaked in just a little bit of rum. But don't you worry, there's a nonalcoholic version so all can enjoy!

PREP TIME: 40 MINUTES • COOKING TIME: 15 MINUTES • SERVES: 2

2 oz (60 g) raisins

¼ to ½ cup (60 to 120 ml) rum or chocolate liquor (see note), plus extra for drizzling

¼ to ⅓ cup (20 to 26 g) gluten-free rolled oats

1 tbsp (12 g) melted butter or coconut oil

1 tsp cinnamon

12 oz (340 g) Greek yogurt

1 tbsp (12 g) coconut sugar

Honey

Preheat the oven to 350°F (177°C). Line a sheet pan with foil or parchment paper.

Place the raisins in enough rum to cover them and soak for 30 minutes or more. The raisins will expand while soaking. After soaking, drain the raisins, reserving the rum.

In a small bowl, combine the oats, melted butter and cinnamon. Place the oat mixture on the lined sheet pan and bake for 12 to 14 minutes.

In a medium bowl, whip the Greek yogurt, coconut sugar and 3 tablespoons (45 ml) of reserved liquid from the soaked raisins until fluffy.

Divide the yogurt mixture evenly between 2 serving bowls. Add the toasted oat mixture followed by the rum-soaked raisins. Drizzle with the rum, chocolate liquor or honey.

Note: For the non-alcoholic version of soaked raisins, soak the raisins in water with 1 to 2 teaspoons (5 to 10 ml) rum extract. Replace the chocolate liquor with melted dark chocolate or chocolate sauce.

BLUEBERRIES 'N CREAM BOWLS

This day and age, food allergies are very common. It can be hard to accommodate everyone's dietary needs as well. I can relate to many of these food-allergy dilemmas, and it's another reason why I love creating delicious allergy-free food. Two of my favorite Paleo and vegan dessert substitutes to use are cashew cream and coconut cream. Both are amazing replacements for real cream and do wonders in a dessert bowl like this. Enjoy a simple new way to eat dessert!

PREP TIME: 24 HOURS • COOKING TIME: 0 MINUTES • SERVES: 2

½ cup (120 ml) coconut cream

⅓ cup (40 g) cashews

Purified water

2 cups (300 g) frozen blueberries

1 tsp vanilla

Maple syrup or Xylitol sweetener, to taste

Pinch of ginger

Toasted nuts

Dark chocolate shavings

Fresh mint, for garnish

Coconut milk, for topping

Chill the canned coconut cream in the fridge for 24 hours to thicken. Drain the excess liquid and discard.

To soak the cashews, cover them in purified water for 2 hours. After soaking, discard all but 1 to 2 tablespoons (15 to 30 ml) of cashew water.

In a blender or food processor, combine the chilled coconut cream, soaked cashews, frozen berries, vanilla, maple syrup and ginger. Blend well and scrape the sides often, making sure to blend all of the big chunks. If the mixture is too thick to churn, add a splash of liquefied coconut milk.

Pour the blended berries and cream mixture into 2 small bowls.

Top with the toasted nuts, dark chocolate shavings and garnish with mint. For an extra-creamy version, add an additional splash of coconut milk on top of each bowl.

MEXICAN CHOCOLATE ALMOND NICE CREAM BOWL

Have you ever heard of nice cream? It's basically frozen bananas that you churn into a soft serve. Yes, it's very nice to your waistline, nice to food allergies and nice to taste. Consider that your excuse to make a second bowl now, right? You'll get a boost of antioxidants with vitamin E–rich almonds and 100% dark chocolate. Not to mention a healthy dose of potassium from all those nice bananas.

PREP TIME: 1 HOUR, 10 MINUTES • COOKING TIME: 0 MINUTES • SERVES: 1

BOWLS
1 to 2 tbsp (12 to 24 g) almond butter or peanut butter

2 bananas, frozen

1 tbsp (15 ml) dark chocolate, melted

1 to 2 tbsp (7 to 14 g) cocoa powder

Pinch of cinnamon

Pinch of cayenne pepper

Pinch of fine sea salt or kosher salt

1 tsp vanilla extract

TOPPINGS
1 tbsp (11 g) toasted almonds

1 tbsp (15 ml) dark chocolate sauce or melted dark chocolate

1 tbsp (8 g) gluten-free granola, optional

1 tbsp (5 g) unsweetened shredded coconut

Cinnamon

Freeze the almond butter in 1 or 2 ice cube slots in an ice cube tray for 45 minutes to 1 hour. If you're planning on using a blender, don't freeze the almond butter beforehand, as it will not blend well.

In a food processor or blender, combine the almond butter, bananas, melted dark chocolate, cocoa powder, cinnamon, cayenne pepper, salt and vanilla. Process for 2 to 3 minutes. Stop and scrape the sides and continue processing until a soft-serve texture is formed. This will take several blending cycles, and it helps to give the food processor a rest to prevent overheating.

Pour into 1 small serving bowl. Top with the almonds, dark chocolate sauce, gluten-free granola, if desired, shredded coconut and a pinch of cinnamon.

PEANUT BUTTER COOKIE DOUGH PARFAIT BOWLS

What's not to love about cookie dough? This cookie dough version is actually a no-bake cookie dough bite recipe from my blog and loved by many. I wanted to keep that love going so I included those little bites as a topping for this perfectly parfait yogurt bowl. It's deceptively healthy and delicious!

PREP TIME: 40 MINUTES • COOKING TIME: 30 MINUTES • SERVES: 2

COOKIE DOUGH BITES (SEE NOTES)

¾ cup (60 g) gluten-free quick oats or gluten-free cereal of choice

½ cup (50 g) almond flour or peanut flour

¼ cup (30 g) vanilla protein powder

½ tbsp (4 g) cinnamon

¼ to ⅓ cup (45 to 60 g) salted creamy peanut butter (creamy no-stir works best)

¼ to ⅓ cup (45 to 60 ml) maple syrup or honey

1 tsp vanilla

BOWLS

1 cup (245 g) Greek yogurt (see notes)

2 tbsp (25 g) creamy peanut butter

1 tbsp (15 ml) honey

½ cup (80 g) chopped honey nuts, maple nuts or roasted cinnamon nuts

¼ cup (20 g) toasted coconut

1 to 2 tbsp (15 to 30 ml) molasses

Sprinkle of coconut sugar

Pinch of sea salt

To make the cookie dough bites, grind up the oats in a food processor and transfer them to a mixing bowl. Add the almond flour, protein powder, cinnamon and peanut butter. Stir the ingredients, mixing well.

Add the maple syrup and vanilla, then mix again with your hands. You might need to add more maple syrup or nut butter if the batter gets too dry. Roll into 1- to 1½-inch (2.5- to 3-cm) balls and place on a parchment paper lined cookie tray. Freeze the cookie dough balls for 20 to 30 minutes, then transfer to a Ziploc bag until ready to use.

For the bowls, whisk the yogurt, peanut butter and honey in a medium-size bowl. Keep in 1 bowl or divide into 2 individual bowls. Top with the nuts, crumbled cookie dough bites and toasted coconut. Drizzle with the molasses and sprinkle with the coconut sugar and sea salt.

Notes: Don't worry, if you don't have time to make the cookie dough bites, these parfait bowls are great with just peanut butter cookies crumbled on top. Udi's gluten-free makes a great gluten-free and dairy-free coconut peanut butter cookie!

The cookie dough bites recipe makes at least 15 to 16 bites. It's one of my favorite no-bake bites recipes so you will be happy to have extra!

For a dairy-free option, replace the Greek yogurt with nondairy yogurt or whipped chilled coconut cream (see page 154 for the coconut whip recipe).

GREEK GODDESS COCOA BOWL

Fresh figs, food of the gods, are packed with potassium, calcium, fiber and a lot more divine health benefits. So now you see why I'm calling this a Greek goddess dessert bowl, right? The combination of rich dark chocolate, toasted ancient grains and figs will definitely leave you feeling like a goddess. That's a good thing, so eat up!

PREP TIME: 35 MINUTES • COOKING TIME: 5 TO 6 MINUTES • SERVES: 1 TO 2

½ cup (85 g) dried figs, stems removed

1 to 1½ cups (240 to 355 ml) purified water

¼ to ⅓ cup (45 to 60 g) buckwheat groats

2 to 3 tsp (5 to 7 g) cocoa powder, unsweetened

2 tsp (10 ml) coconut oil

1 tbsp (12 g) coconut sugar or brown sugar

1 medium banana (fresh or frozen)

1¼ cups (310 g) Greek yogurt, plain or vanilla (see note)

Cocoa nibs or dark chocolate chips

Extra cocoa powder, optional

Preheat the oven to 350°F (177°C).

Soak the figs in water for 30 minutes to soften. Soaking will expand the figs and create a smoother texture for the dessert bowls. Discard the water after soaking. Slice the soaked figs and set aside.

In a small bowl, combine the buckwheat groats with the cocoa powder, coconut oil and sugar, mixing well. Spread the coated buckwheat groats on a cookie sheet and toast for 5 to 6 minutes. Remove from the oven and set aside.

In a blender, combine the banana and yogurt, blending well. For an extra-thick consistency, use a frozen banana.

Pour the banana and yogurt mixture into a serving bowl and top with the cocoa crispy toasted buckwheat and sliced figs. Top with the cocoa nibs or dark chocolate chips. Feel free to add a bit of dark cocoa powder for dusting, if desired.

Note: For dairy-free option, use nondairy yogurt or whipped chilled coconut cream (see page 154).

ACKNOWLEDGMENTS

I can't believe I just wrote a cookbook. In all honesty, I was terrified. But I decided to embrace the fear as long as there was three times as much passion to overshadow it. A huge thank you and hug to my readers, my family and Page Street Publishing for keeping that passion alive and thriving! You all truly inspired me.

Thank you to my husband for being patient with me and supporting me throughout this whole journey. I couldn't have done it without you testing and tasting over 100 different recipes. I'm so happy you like to eat, haha!

Thank you to my parents for always believing in me 1,000%! Thank you for your love and for always saying you were proud of me. It was the confidence I needed to keep going toward my dreams.

Thank you to my dear friends Laurie Messer and Brooke Lark. You two are true angels. Thank you both for your generosity and encouraging me each step of the way. What a blessing!

And lastly, thank you to my all my amazing readers and friends, from years past to now. I've been blogging for a long time, so you know who you are! And I have probably emailed with you at least once. I love that! I love staying connected and being there for each other. Thank you for allowing me to take my passion and turn it into print.

To the person who purchased this book, THANK YOU! My heart and soul are in the recipes and I hope they bring you good health, and joy as well.

ABOUT THE AUTHOR

Lindsay Cotter is the gluten-free nutrition specialist, full-time recipe developer and food photographer at the blog Cotter Crunch. As a wife to a former pro athlete, her focus is on good food, good fuel and feeding active people with delicious, gluten-free recipes. Not to mention providing a lot of great nutrition discussion!

She started blogging to share healthy easy recipes that helped fuel her then–pro athlete husband, as well as recipes that helped her recover from personal health issues. She now uses her site to support and guide others struggling with food allergies or eating gluten-free in general.

Lindsay is passionate about working with whole-foods-based brands and helping others find a real food diet that specifically works for them.

Her recipes have been featured in *Shape* magazine, *Good Housekeeping*, *Self* magazine, *Low-Sugar Living* magazine, *Men's Fitness*, *Triathlete* magazine, *Fitness* magazine, *Women's Health* and Primal Palate.

She currently lives in Austin, Texas, with her husband and chocolate lab, Sadie. They enjoy hiking trails and hitting all the funky coffee shops.

INDEX